Keskidee

Teacher's Guide 4

Ann Ward, Anne Worrall, Emma Derrick,
Yvonne Forde, Laurel Ince and Neville Grant

LONGMAN

Publishing for the Caribbean

Published by Addison Wesley Longman Limited
Edinburgh Gate, Harlow,
Essex CM20 2JE, England
and Associated Companies throughout the world

Lexicon Trinidad Limited,
Boundary Road, San Juan, Trinidad

Carlong Publishers (Caribbean) Limited,
P.O. Box 489, 33 Second Street,
Newport West, Kingston 13, Jamaica

First published 1997

ISBN 0 582 24676 8

Produced by Longman Asia Limited, Hong Kong.
NPCC/01

Project team

Ann Ward	Anne Worrall
Emma Derrick	Yvonne Forde	Laurel Ince

Advisory panel

The Publishers would like to thank the
following teachers and teacher trainers for their
invaluable guidance and ideas at a series of
workshops, out of which grew Keskidee
Integrated Language Arts for the Caribbean.

Dayanand Bhagirath	Yvonne Isaac
Arlene Black	Grace King
Raffiena Boodoosingh	Cindy Ramkallawa
Pamela Boxhill	Rae Samuel
Kitts Cadette	Joseph Sanchez
Allison Douglas	Brenda Shah
Rosamond Estrada	Joyce Spencer
Priscilla George	Colleen Thornton

Contents

Notes on using this guide

1 Cross references

Unless otherwise stated, all cross-references made in the text of this guide – for example, *see page 22* – are to pages in this guide, not to the Pupils' Book or Workbook. References to these books mention the book in question – for example, *see page 26 of Workbook 4.*

Page references in the margins of the sections that provide detailed commentary on the Pupils' Book and the Workbook are to the book commented on. For example:

> **WB4** **3**
> **PAGE**
> **5** Ask the children to work in pairs to complete the table. Check the answers with the class.
>
> **Answers:** American, Jamaican, French, Spanish, Danish, Mexican, Trinidadian.

refers to *Workbook 4*, page 5

and

> **PB4** **5**
> **PAGE**
> **4** Read and discuss the guidelines for making a storybook with the class. Ask the children to start contents pages and decorate the covers of their own story books. Revise the instructions for writing a story given on page 3 of the Pupils' Book, and go through the stages as the children write their own stories.
>   Read and discuss the children's stories.

refers to *Pupils' Book 4*, page 4.

2 The phonetic alphabet

A phonetic alphabet is not used in this guide, but reference to phonetic characters is made by using a solidus (/) either side of a normal alphabetic character. Thus, 'g' in the text of this guide refers to the written character, which may have a varying sound (for example, hard in *ghost* and *garden*, soft in *gem* and *giant*), whereas /g/ refers only to the phonetic hard g sound as in *gate*, *ghastly*, *glove*, *goat*, *green*, *guitar*, etc.

Introduction to the Keskidee course

Keskidee is a complete language course which takes children through the entire infant and primary school syllabus. It starts with the child's very first steps in learning to read and write, and finishes with the complex skills required for the Common Entrance Examination, or other final-year assessments. The course provides continuity and a spiral progression, incorporating constant revision. This ensures that children acquire the language proficiency they need for secondary schooling and for their lives outside school.

Structure

The vital first year

In *Keskidee* great importance is attached to the early infant years. If children fall behind at this stage, it is very difficult for them to catch up later. This course ensures that children are given a solid foundation in the basic skills of listening, speaking, reading and writing. To this end we have designed three workbooks for the first year of the course. They provide young children with practice in basic phonics, letter formation and word-building, which is essential for later language development. The workbooks ensure that the children are actively developing skills; they are 'learning by doing', which is more effective than passive learning.

Also for this year, we have designed six classroom resources posters and an introductory reader – *Pupils' Book 1*.

Solid development through the middle years

After the first year, the course follows a regular format of one pupils' book and one workbook per year. Language content and skills are developed gradually, with constant revision of what has gone before.

The final years (Year 6, and, in some countries, Year 7)

The final level of this course – the Pupils' Book and Workbook for Year 6 – has been specially designed to prepare children for the Common Entrance Exam, or other final-year assessments. The Pupils' Book contains a clear and concise summary of all the main grammatical points, and can therefore be used as a reference book for revision purposes. The Workbook provides revision exercises and practice in examination questions. This level has been so designed that it can be used for two terms (in countries with six-year primary school systems) or five terms (for countries with seven-year systems). Teachers will see how to use this level for their own systems, and the Teacher's Guide will help them to plan for this important stage.

An integrated course (grammar in context)

Keskidee is an integrated language course where the skills of listening, reading, comprehension, grammar, spelling and composition are taught and practised hand in hand. Rules of grammar and spelling are set out clearly. Pupils are immediately asked to put these rules into practice as a means of expressing their thoughts, ideas and opinions in oral discussion or written composition. This avoids the problem of pupils writing grammatically correct sentences in grammar lessons, but failing to apply this knowledge to other forms of writing.

Cross-curricular topics

Language items in *Keskidee* are always presented in context, never as isolated examples. These contexts cover a wide variety of exciting topics, both factual and fictional, from calypsoes to coral reefs, and heroes to hurricanes. The topics are chosen specifically to motivate young children. They also link with other subjects in the curriculum, notably Social Studies, Science – and also Technology and Environmental Awareness. Maths is, of course, included in activities such as counting.

A love of reading, and an appreciation of literature

From the very beginning of the course, children are introduced to simple poems and extracts from stories, to stimulate their interest in literature and to encourage an early love of reading.

To accompany the course there is also a graded reading series, the *Read Awhile* series. This series is not essential to the language course, but is highly recommended as extended reading practice. The series includes both fiction and non-fiction, and the children will love reading the books. See the section at the end of this guide for further information about this series.

Assessment

The *Keskidee* course includes regular assessment activities throughout. These will help to familiarise children with tests and assessments, and will help teachers to identify areas of difficulty for some children so that reinforcement activities or remedial work can be given.

Guidance for teachers

The *Keskidee* teacher's guides (one per year) are packed with ideas and extra activities, providing invaluable support for busy teachers. They contain suggestions for practical teaching aids, simple crafts, stories, songs and rhymes related to the lessons in the pupils' books. They also contain matrices that show the skills and contents for the entire course. This provides a quick reference for teachers, and will help them to match the course to the syllabus requirements.

Keskidee aims to encourage pupils and teachers to see language as the key that opens the door to an exciting world of opportunity, knowledge and enjoyment.

Your views are important

The course has benefited greatly from the expertise and ideas of teachers throughout the Caribbean. The project team, and the publishers, are indebted to them for their help, and hope that many more teachers will comment on the course as they make use of it. We would welcome all comments and suggestions – things you liked, things you didn't, and new ideas for activities – and will consider them carefully for new editions in the future. The address to write to is: The Keskidee Publisher, International Department, Addison Wesley Longman Limited, Edinburgh Gate, Harlow, Essex CM20 2JE, England.

Keskidee Year One Scheme of work

Listening and speaking	Language structure	Reading	Writing	Concepts
Workbook 1a				
Listening: to the teacher, to one another, to stories Identifying sounds	**Verb:** *to be*	**Pre-reading** Matching pictures, shapes and words	**Pre-writing** **Tracing and copying:** patterns, shapes and letters	Categorisation
Telling a story from pictures	**Verb tenses:** present continuous, present simple	Sequencing patterns and pictures		Sequence Fact and fantasy Road safety The past
Asking questions		**Phonics:** all initial sounds	Formation of all lower-case letters	
Saying where things are	**Prepositions:** *in, on, under*			Position
Describing colour, shape, animals, etc	Adjectives			Size Shape Colour
Workbook 1b				
Listening: to stories, rhymes and riddles	Apostrophe 's' ('s) for possession	Finding rhyming words	Copying words	Rhythm and music
Comparing sounds	Comparative adjectives	Word and picture matching	Formation of all capital letters	Number
Counting 1-10	Plural 's'	Word building	Numerals 1-10	Alphabet
Chanting the alphabet		Telling a story from pictures	Pluralisation	Fear
Saying what they can do	**Auxiliary verbs:** *can, must*		Writing own name	Names
Talking about the past	Past simple tense		Supplying initial letters	The past
Workbook 1c				
Listening: to stories, songs and rhymes, to riddles, to music	Possessive adjectives	Sentence building with flashcards	Filling in gaps in sentences	Music
	Comparative and superlative adjectives	Matching pictures and captions	Copying words and captions	
Comparing sounds	**Verb:** *to have*			Pets
Expressing likes and dislikes	Opposites	Medial vowels	Sentence building	Food and nutrition
		Final consonants		Opposites
Expressing feelings	**Sentences:** capital letter and full stop			Family
Retelling stories	Future tense			Emotions
Acting out stories				Safety on the beach
Predicting endings				Role play
				Imagination

Keskidee Year Two Scheme of work

Topics	Listening and speaking	Language structure	Reading	Writing	Other skills
Social Studies Friends Personal identity Family Helping at home Past and present Homes Leisure and sport **Science** Insects Colour Teeth Hygiene Weather Twins Conservation Endangered species **Literature** Books Folktales	**Listening:** to the teacher, to one another **Listening:** to stories, poems, rhymes, riddles Retelling stories Discussing characters Predicting the outcome Role play Asking and answering questions Giving and following verbal instructions Relating own experiences Expressing feelings Expressing opinions Comparing past and present Word games Inventing new words	**Verbs:** *to be, to have* **Tenses:** present simple, present continuous, past simple, present perfect Sentences Questions Negatives Plural 's' and some irregulars **Adjectives:** possessives, comparatives and superlatives, opposites Similes **Nouns:** proper and common Gender Apostrophe 's' ('s) Homophones Compound words	**Phonics:** initial and final consonants, medial vowels, consonant blends and digraphs, magic 'e' **Comprehension:** matching pictures and captions, verbal reasoning, multiple-choice comprehension questions **Information:** captions and labels; instructions for exercises, games, projects; lists and rotas; timetables; book titles **Enjoyment:** stories, poems, puzzles, jokes; dialogues for role play; word games	**Punctuation:** capitals, full stops and question marks, apostrophe 's' ('s) Simple descriptions of people, animals, toys Writing captions Labelling diagrams Telling stories from pictures Giving simple instructions Keeping a simple diary Messages on cards Addresses Writing a letter to a friend Simple book review Dialogue for role play Wordplay – alliteration Crosswords and word games Handwriting practice	Working with partner/group Alphabetical order Making a picture dictionary Cataloguing books Using a library Using reference books to find information Differentiating fact and fiction Organising simple project work Categorising Correcting own mistakes Making a weather chart Reading simple plans Designing and giving instructions for making a model from junk Making simple puppets for role play

Keskidee Year Three Scheme of work

Topics	Listening and speaking	Language structure	Reading	Writing	Other skills

Topics

Social Studies
- Festivals and customs
- Emergency services
- Litter
- Maps
- Countries of the world
- Holidays
- Studying strategies
- Newspapers

Science
- Sound
- Plants
- Rainforests
- Conservation
- Camouflage
- Space travel
- Whales

Other
- Cricket
- Legends

Listening and speaking
- Asking and answering questions
- Conducting an interview
- Reporting an event
- Relating own experiences
- Retelling a story
- Dramatising a story
- Role play
- Giving and following verbal instructions
- Making a phone call
- Listening to and describing sounds
- Listening to and appreciating the rhythm and sounds of poetry
- Expressing hopes and wishes
- Expressing opinions
- Making moral judgements

Language structure
- Verbs
- **Verb tenses:** present simple, present continuous, past simple, present perfect, future
- **Adjectives:** opposites, synonyms, comparatives and superlatives (using *more/most*)
- **Nouns:** proper nouns, nouns from verbs
- Abbreviations
- **Pronouns:** possessive, personal
- Plural apostrophe 's' (s')
- **Conjunctions:** *and, but, because*
- Adverbs
- Prepositions
- Homophones
- *There is/are; was/were*
- Compound words

Reading
- **Phonics:** vowel digraphs, diphthongs, consonant blends, silent letters, rhyming words, onomatopoeic words, alliterative words
- **Comprehension:** multiple choice, comprehension questions, simple inference
- **Information:** newspaper reports; instructions for exercises, projects, games, crafts; biographical notes; grammatical explanations
- **Enjoyment:** Stories, poems, legends, folktales, songs, jokes, puzzles, reading aloud (with sound effects)

Writing
- **Punctuation:** capitals, full stops, question marks, commas in lists, apostrophe 's', ('s)
- **Spelling:** common digraphs, silent 'k'
- Gap-filling exercises
- Answers to comprehension questions
- Reporting events
- Taking notes
- Writing a report from notes
- Relating a story/a real or imaginary experience
- Newspaper articles
- An interview from notes
- Simple descriptions of people and places
- Instructions
- Composing verses for a song
- A simple poem
- A letter to a friend
- Handwriting practice

Other skills
- Making a class newspaper
- Using Contents pages
- Working in a group
- Performing a play
- Sign language (deaf and dumb alphabet)
- Organising project work
- Making a poster
- Map reading
- Improving writing
- Measuring
- Mnemonics
- Correcting mistakes
- Making a calendar
- Identifying flags
- Making models from junk
- Making a collage
- Solving puzzles

Keskidee Year Four Scheme of work

Topics	Listening and speaking	Language structure	Reading	Writing	Other skills
Social Studies Family history Arawaks and Caribs Slavery Bullying Emigration Ambitions Caribbean countries Maps Languages Customs **Science** Food Bush medicine Manatees Parrots Anteaters Conservation Volcanoes Weather **Other** Music and songs Stories, fables and folktales Folklore Art – Cazabon Advertisements	**Listening:** to stories, songs, poems, rhymes Retelling stories Discussing characters and plot Predicting the outcome Role play Describing people, animals and places Asking and answering questions Talking about the past Comparing past and present Relating own experiences Expressing feelings, desires, ambitions Expressing moral judgements, opinions Describing ailments Making hypotheses Describing emotions, fears, likes and dislikes Using imagination Singing songs Word games Telling jokes	Sentences and questions Subject of sentence **Nouns:** proper nouns, collective nouns, abstract nouns, nouns from verbs, nouns from adjectives Plurals (irregular) **Verb tenses:** past simple (regular and irregular), present simple Contractions **Pronouns:** personal, reflexive **Adjectives:** comparative and superlative, adjectives from nouns, opposites Adverbs of manner *Much* and *many* **Prefix:** *dis* Prepositions Synonyms Homophones	Syllabication Rhyming words **Comprehension:** comprehension questions, multiple-choice questions, inference **Information:** non-fiction passages; grammatical explanations; instructions for exercises, projects, compositions, games; captions, labels, maps, family trees; menus, recipes, adverts **Enjoyment:** stories, folktales, fables, poems, song lyrics, dialogues, jokes, word games; reading aloud for pronunciation; appreciating music and poetry	**Punctuation:** capital letters, full stops and question marks, apostrophe 's' (singular and plural) apostrophe in contractions Planning, constructing and revising stories, accounts, reports **Creative writing:** stories, poems, lyrics, dialogue Retelling stories **Descriptions:** people, animals, places, feelings, fears Reporting an event; Writing a description from notes Writing book reviews Writing recipes and menus Extending vocabulary **Spelling rules:** plurals: *y – ies*, *f – ves*; soft 'c' before e/i/y; vowel digraph: *ea*; consonants: *ph* Wordplay – alliteration Crosswords and word games	Working with partner/group Map reading Using a dictionary Using Contents pages Using reference books for projects Making a storybook Musical notation Reading music Appreciating art Assessing own work Correcting mistakes

Keskidee Year Five Scheme of work

Topics	Listening and speaking	Language structure	Reading	Writing	Other skills
Social Studies Heroism Challenges Emigration Visual handicap Carnival Tourism Products of the Caribbean Buccaneers Mayan Indians **Science** Floods Hurricanes Pollution Conservation Planets Ecology **Other** Greek mythology Legends Humour Calypsoes	Relating events and experiences Describing people and places Describing a process Expressing a point of view Making a speech in a class debate Expressing moral judgement Differentiating fact and opinion Telling a story Predicting the outcome Asking for and giving directions Making emergency phone calls Role play Using a dictionary to aid pronunciation Making hypotheses Describing emotions Using imagination Word games Telling jokes	**Verb tenses:** past simple, present perfect, past perfect, present passive, past passive, future passive **Nouns:** abstract, gender, categories Relative pronouns *Both/neither* Prepositions Adverbs of time **Adjectives:** comparative and superlative Synonyms Homophones Metaphors Similes Prefixes and suffixes Word families Relative clauses	Syllabication **Comprehension:** comprehension questions, multiple-choice questions, true or false statements, inferring meaning from context **Information:** reading reference books for information; using an index; using Contents pages; instructions for exercises, projects, games; directions; captions and labels; diagrams; maps and charts; questionnaires **Enjoyment:** stories, folktales, fables, poems, legends, myths, calypsoes, games, jokes	**Punctuation:** speech marks in direct speech Reported speech Abbreviations Summarising main ideas **Descriptions:** a process, people and places Reporting events and experiences Reporting events from different points of view Preparing a speech for debate Giving written instructions Writing biography **Creative writing:** calypsoes, poems, fables, conclusion to a story Writing a letter Filling in forms Spelling rules	Working with partner/group Using reference books, atlas, dictionary, etc Organising project work Empathising with the visually handicapped Reading Braille alphabet Sequencing Reporting events chronologically Designing costumes Self-assessment Using initiative

Keskidee Year Six Scheme of work

Topics	Listening and speaking	Language structure	Reading	Writing	Other skills
Social Studies Personal memories, ambitions, achievements Urban vs rural life Creole dialect Superstition Humour Examinations Board games Television Cinema Amy Johnson **Science** Sharks Coral reefs Water Bushfires Conservation Pollution **Literature** Derek Walcott Samuel Selvon Andrew Salkey	Discussing use of Standard English and Creole dialect Expressing a point of view Deducing Making a speech in a debate Making comparisons Making value judgements Giving reasons for opinions Making suggestions Relating own experiences Talking about past, present and future activities Expressing hopes and ambitions Describing early memories Giving and following instructions Expressing likes and dislikes Describing a process Reporting what someone has said Predicting the outcome of a story	Sentences and phrases Paragraphs **Verb tenses:** present simple, past simple, present continuous, past continuous, future, perfect, past perfect, present passive, past passive, passive/active **Participles:** present, past **Verb agreement:** subject/object/predicate **Adjectives:** comparative and superlative, possessive **Adverbs:** of time, manner and place **Pronouns:** personal, possessive Conjunctions Prepositions **Nouns:** abstract, proper, common, collective Synonyms Antonyms Homonyms Homophones Similes Metaphors Prefixes and suffixes	Word attack skills Deducing meaning from context, prefix, suffix, etc **Comprehension:** comprehension questions, multiple-choice questions, true/false statements Explanations of points of grammar **Information:** descriptions of processes, instructions, biographical notes, newspaper report, magazine article, TV programme schedule, film review **Enjoyment:** literary extracts, poems, fables, Creole dialect Suggestions for wider reading Appreciating imagery in prose and poetry	Punctuation Paragraphs Planning, constructing and revising a composition Improving own writing Correcting own mistakes Direct and indirect speech **Descriptions:** people, places, events, scenes, TV programmes Relating own experiences Instructions for board games A film review A letter **Creative writing:** stories, poems Using imagery to enhance writing Filling in charts	Working with partner/group Using a dictionary Using an index Self-assessment Preparing for examinations Recognising self-worth Persuading others to own point of view

Introduction to Year 4

What kind of course is Keskidee?

Keskidee is an integrated language course which:

- focuses on the skills children need to use English effectively
- helps busy teachers to plan exciting, effective lessons
- helps teachers to create a non-threatening environment for learning
- enables children to develop a positive attitude to learning
- is fun to use, for teachers and pupils.

Keskidee is an integrated language course which includes the development of oral English and grammar alongside reading and writing skills. Thus, while a lot of attention is given to the basic skills of reading and writing, children are encouraged to use oral English to talk about the topics of the lessons – making what they see, hear and read about part of their own experience.

An integrated approach is now the recommended method of teaching language arts across the Caribbean. Teachers who are not currently using this method can use the Keskidee course to phase in this approach.

The topics have been chosen to interest young children and because they relate to other subjects in the curriculum.

What is the Year 4 course designed to do?

Some of the things that the Year 4 course has been designed to do are:

- to encourage the children to talk and express themselves clearly in Standard English
- to develop a wider English vocabulary
- to develop concepts necessary for learning, e.g. categorising, sequencing, predicting

- to develop reading and writing skills
- to develop an awareness of basic grammatical structures, tenses and parts of speech
- to stimulate an interest in books and encourage a love of literature
- to provide opportunities for assessment and evaluation
- to teach and practise spelling
- to continue the development of handwriting skills.

What kind of help does this Teacher's Guide provide?

The Teacher's Guide gives support and suggestions for busy teachers on how to use the Keskidee course components, and how to supplement them with additional activities to provide extra practice in all the basic skills.

What are the Keskidee course components for Year 4?

The Year Four course has the following components:

- a pupils' book (*Pupils' Book 4*)
- a workbook (*Workbook 4*)
- a teacher's guide (*Teacher's Guide 4*)

Using the pupils' book

The pupils' book introduces new topics, organised as 20 units. Each unit includes reading passages, reading comprehension exercises, introduction of grammar points, spelling, compositions, projects, games, jokes or songs. The topics in the pupils' book are themselves designed to be used as a springboard for oral work and other activities. There are three assessment units in the pupils' book. They appear after Units 7, 14 and 20.

Using the workbook

The workbook exercises give extra practice, particularly in written work. Most exercises can be done by the children working either on their own or in pairs, with some guidance from the teachers. Others can more usefully be done as classwork. Like many of the exercises in the pupils' book, the workbook exercises can be used as stimuli for oral work and other activities (these are suggested in this guide).

The Keskidee 'icons'

So that the children may instantly recognise the kind of exercise that they are being asked to do, the Pupils' Book and Workbook at Keskidee level 2 introduced a series of 'icons' that make use of the Keskidee bird motif. These icons are intended to reinforce the exercise rubric that tells the children what to do — read, practise some spelling, write a composition, etc. The children will have already familiarised themselves with these icons, and they will encounter them again in levels 5 and 6.

Six different icons are used, as follows:

 denotes an activity to practise oral English

 denotes an activity to practise spelling

 denotes an activity to practise writing

 denotes an activity to practise reading

 denotes a rhyme, a riddle or a joke

 denotes a game

How do I put it all together?

The course for Year 4 has been divided into 20 units in both the Pupils' Book and the Workbook and three assessment units (in the Pupils' Book). The workbook exercises can be done at the teacher's convenience, to reinforce the work of the Pupils' Book.

The main section of the Teacher's Guide (starting at page 19) includes the objectives for each unit, suggestions for using the course materials to realise these objectives, and suggestions for other activities which can be used or adapted to complement the published material.

The notes for each unit are preceded by a page that summarises that unit's objectives. A sample section of such a page is shown at the top of the next page.

This page summarises the content of the unit, and is followed by page-by-page suggestions for using the exercises in the Pupils' Book and the Workbook, and suggestions for other activities (projects, games, role plays, etc) that can be used to supplement and enrich the published material.

Of course, it would hardly be possible to take up all the suggestions for other activities, but they provide a useful base of ideas which teachers can use or adapt.

Working straight through the Pupils' Book and Workbook in sequence will provide an integrated course. The objectives pages at the beginning of each unit in the Teacher's Guide show the learning strategies divided into skill sections. If teachers wish, they can use this as a guide and teach the skills separately.

Reading	Reading a passage about stories	PB page 1
	Answering questions about the passage	PB1, WB1
	Reading instructions	PB4, PB5
Spelling	Spelling check	Ac6
Writing	Writing answers to questions	PB2
	Planning, writing and revising a story	PB5, WB3, Ac2
	Writing from dictation	Ac5

KEY (All references relate to sections in this unit of the Teacher's Guide)

PB2 = Activity 2 of Unit 1 in *Pupils' Book 4*

WB3 = Activity 3 of Unit 1 in *Workbook 4*

Ac1 = Activity 1 in the *Activities and teaching aids* section of this unit

General suggestions

1 Evaluation and assessment

The assessment units will help you to keep track of the children's progress. Charts similar to the one below will help you to record the children's progress and identify problem areas for the whole class or for individual children.

2 Oral work: eliciting answers

It may sometimes be difficult to get children to speak. It is important to create an atmosphere in which children feel encouraged to speak. It would not be inappropriate occasionally to allow the children to chorus answers to questions: "Who was the richest man in Karika, everybody?"

Over-correcting use of the vernacular can be inhibiting and confusing for young children, so do not discourage shy children from responding in whatever way makes them feel comfortable.

Term: 1

Gradually, correct by repeating the sentence in Standard English: "That's right. Anteaters eat ants." Try to make the clear distinction between correct information (which should be praised, however expressed) and Standard English expression of the information (which children will gradually learn to imitate). After a time, you can start occasionally to ask children to repeat the Standard English model:

Teacher: That's right. Anteaters eat ants. What do anteaters eat?

Children: Anteaters eat ants.

Questions which need *yes* or *no* answers ("Is this a manatee?" "Is it a bird?") are good for a warm-up activity and are easy for shy children to respond to. Gradually encourage children to answer more open questions and answer more fully, e.g.

"Who is Michel Jean Cazabon?"

"He was a painter."

"What is your favourite painting? Why?"

The last question is more demanding, and allows children to explore and express their personal opinions. It should only be asked after the children have had a lot of practice in speaking and answering questions.

Don't forget to refer to children's own experiences:

"Hope went to England. Have you ever been to England? When did you go? Where did you fly to?"

Repeat familiar questions. This is a good way to start a lesson, and it gives children the chance to shine the second time around.

3 Grouping classes for oral work

It is important that all the children can see and hear what is going on and are placed so that they can join in activities such as talking about a picture or telling a story. This can be difficult when space is limited, but it may be possible sometimes to work out of doors or to group the children around you, sitting on the floor.

4 Games

Various games appear in the Pupils' Book and the Teacher's Guide. The games described are relevant and useful, because they relate to the topics in the Pupils' Book and Workbook, and because they develop various learning skills (for example, memory, listening to instructions, guessing, sorting or counting).

Once the children have learned to play a game, it can be played over and over again. Games can also be adapted to cover different teaching points.

5 Planning a lesson

Each lesson should contain a variety of activities. Some activities tend to enliven children, others to quieten them down. After a spell of hard work, children need to do something like a song, a game or a rhyme to end the lesson.

Build into lessons the chance for children to repeat activities, especially those that children found taxing the first time around.

Suggested approaches – a skeleton lesson plan

- *Beginning the lesson – revision of last lesson, preparation for this lesson* (oral work)
- *Presentation of new material* (use real objects or pictures)
- *Main activity or activities* (Pupils' Book or Workbook exercises)
- *Validation* (review presentation material – ask more probing questions) (look at and talk about children's work with the whole class)
- *Ending the lesson* (song, game or rhyme)

6 Adapting Keskidee materials to different learning abilities

Making activities easier
At this stage, the more able children will be able to do the exercises by themselves after being given an example by the teacher. The less able children will need more guidance. Within an exercise there are several steps that can be undertaken, with more or less help from the teacher, although some of these could be omitted. Extra steps to make the activity easier are shown below in **bold**.

- *Discussion of the topic*
Talk about the pictures, if any.

- *Introduce the task*
Make sure that the children understand what they have to do.
Do part of the task orally, using the board if necessary.
Write the answers on the board for the children to copy.

- *Do the task*
The children read, write or do whatever is required.
Break the task up. Do the parts of the task one by one.
The children work in pairs or groups to do the task.
Help children who have difficulties with the task.
Make a note of any problems.

- *Check the work*
Look at the children's work individually.
Read words or sentences aloud with the whole class.

- *Give extra practice*
Some children will need more practice, especially with handwriting. Prepare extra worksheets with sentences for them to copy.

For brighter children, you could extend the range of the activity and ask them to do things on their own. For example, they could draw their own pictures and write about them or read a book on a related topic.

7 Listening activities

Various listening activities are suggested in the Teacher's Guide. These include listening to a story, listening to and following instructions, games that involve listening, e.g. *I Spy*.

It is of course important that all the children in the class should be able to hear what is going on. For storytelling or reading, the children could be grouped in a semi-circle at the front of the class or outside.

The children should also be encouraged always to listen to one other. Asking children questions about what their classmates have said ("What's . . .'s favourite food?") can be helpful in this context. Remind children that repeating something that somebody else has already said is not a proper answer, for example: ". . . gave us the adjective 'spicy'. Can you think of another adjective to use about food?"

8 Pair work or group work

In the Pupils' Book and the Teacher's Guide it is often recommended that the children work in pairs or groups. This is so that they can practise oral English through answering questions, dialogues and role plays. They can also read aloud together.

There are many advantages in encouraging children to work together (for example, it enables them to obtain the maximum oral practice from the time available), although this may not be convenient in every classroom. It would be helpful, however, if the children could work in pairs or groups for part of the lesson. They could have regular partners or groups to work with, or they could occasionally work with different children.

9 Teaching grammar

The scheme of work matrix (page 7) and the objectives for each unit list the grammar points to be taught in each unit. These grammar points will be reintroduced and amplified in Years Five and Six. In Year Four the emphasis is still on grammar in use, and the children should not be overburdened with explanations. Practise using the grammar in sentences that the children can understand and relate to – sentences about themselves and their lives at home and at school are particularly useful. For example, to practise the simple past tense (Unit 3), ask questions about what the children did yesterday: "What did you do yesterday?" or about an incident that happened in the recent past: "Who came here last week? What happened?" Write the children's answers on the board, underlining the past tense verbs: We <u>played</u> cricket.

Ample and frequent practice in a variety of contexts is more valuable at this early stage than detailed explanation.

10 Children's storybooks

The Year Four course introduces the idea of a personal storybook to be written by each child (see Unit 1). This can be an ordinary exercise book, kept specially for the purpose. The Pupils' Book and Teacher's Guide give step-by-step instructions for writing compositions. Thorough preparation, by discussing the topic and planning the composition, is recommended.

The children should also be encouraged to read each other's writing and share their compositions by reading aloud. However, be sensitive to those accounts which may involve very personal or private feelings – for example, the subject of bullying, which may arise out of Unit 11.

11 Projects

Throughout the Pupils' Book there are suggestions for projects for the children to do, linked to the topics of the units. These could be craft projects or could involve finding out more about the topic.

The projects will necessarily involve some preparatory work, such as assembling craft materials or arranging access to reference materials.

12 The mini-dictionary

There is a mini-dictionary on page 92 of *Pupils' Book 4*. Encourage the children to use this to find the meanings of some of the more difficult words in the text.

13 Irregular verb list

There is also a list of common irregular verbs on page 91 of *Pupils' Book 4*, which can be used for reference.

14 Map of the Caribbean

Many of the passages in *Pupils' Book 4* are linked with specific parts of the Caribbean. They are intended to heighten the children's awareness of the various islands and countries.

Instructions are given in the Pupils' Book for labelling and colouring places on the map of the Caribbean in the back of the Workbook. This activity could be linked with a project about the place.

15 Dictations

As a listening and writing activity, dictations have been introduced at this level. These provide a way of checking the childrens' understanding, spelling and listening ability.

16 Reading activities

The section that begins on page 89 discusses reading and using the Longman *Read Awhile* books, which have been specially written for young children in the Caribbean. It is important to introduce children to the world of books, and to give them as much exposure as possible to books they will enjoy. This section gives useful instructions for exploiting books inside and outside the classroom.

As well as the *Read Awhile* books, look out for books which are suitable for this age group and books which match the interests of your class. Try to bring to the class a selection of books with attractive pictures and interesting stories which will motivate the children to learn to read. If a story or a book captures the children's imagination, build on the interest aroused by planning other activities, e.g. drawing or acting out a scene from the story.

Teaching the Units

OBJECTIVES OF THIS UNIT
- to develop the children's reading skills
- to encourage them to talk about stories
- to encourage them to use their imagination to tell a story
- to teach them the structure underlying good storywriting

Language skill area	Teaching/learning strategies	Where found
Speaking and listening	Discussing a reading passage	PB1
	Telling a story	PB3, WB3, Ac3, Ac4
	Dictation	Ac5
	Relating a story from pictures	WB3
Grammar	Using punctuation in sentences	PB4, WB4
Reading	Reading a passage about stories	PB page 1
	Answering questions about the passage	PB1, WB1
	Reading instructions	PB4, PB5
Spelling	Spelling check	Ac6
Writing	Writing answers to questions	PB2
	Planning, writing and revising a story	PB5, WB3, Ac2
	Writing from dictation	Ac5

KEY (All references relate to sections in this unit of the Teacher's Guide)

PB2   =   Activity 2 of Unit 1 in *Pupils' Book 4*

WB3   =   Activity 3 of Unit 1 in *Workbook 4*

Ac1   =   Activity 1 in the *Activities and teaching aids* section of this unit

Using the Pupils' Book

PB4 PAGE 1 Discuss stories with the class. Ask: *What kind of stories do you like best? Do you like stories about animals? Can you think of a story about animals? Can you think of a funny story? Can you think of a scary story? Why is it frightening?* etc. Elicit the titles of favourite stories and ask what they are about.

Ask the children to read the passage on page 1 on their own.

PB4 PAGE 2 **1**

Read and discuss the questions with the class. Ask the children to find the sentences in the reading passage which give the answers to the questions.

2

Ask the children to write their answers in their books as full sentences, then read and check them, working in pairs. Go over the answers again orally with the class before correcting the children's writing.

3

Read the instructions and explain the activity. Make sure the class is seated in such a way that all the children can hear what is happening and join in. As the class tell the story, ask questions for clarification, and ask the children to summarise the story so far: *Did he make a noise when he ...? What kind of noise do you think he made? So the woman disappeared and then you noticed that ...*

PB4 PAGE 3 **4**

Read and discuss the guidelines with the class. Use examples to illustrate points from the instructions. For example, read the beginning of a story and ask: *Do you think this story starts in an interesting way? Does it make you want to read the rest of the story? What are the words that make you want to find out about the rest of the story?*

PB4 PAGE 4 **5**

Read and discuss the guidelines for making a storybook with the class. Ask the children to start contents pages and decorate the covers of their own story books. Revise the instructions for writing a story given on page 3 of the Pupils' Book, and go through the stages as the children write their own stories.

Read and discuss the children's stories. Invite individual children to read their stories to the class.

When you evaluate the children's stories, take into account all the points mentioned in this unit. Make the distinction between the ability to write a good story and the mechanical factors – spelling, punctuation, grammar and handwriting – but make sure that the children understand that both are important.

Using the Workbook

WB4 PAGE 1 **1**

Ask the children to do the crossword to practise using the vocabulary featured on page 1 of the Pupils' Book, working on their own or in pairs. Check the answers with the class.
Answers: Down: spiderman
Across: 1 story, 2 picture, 3 rings, 4 radio, 5 cover, 6 rocks, 7 album, 8 tale, 9 funny.

2

Ask the children to work on their own or in pairs to find and draw lines to the items named. Go over the answers with the class.

WB4 PAGE 2 **3**

The children can tell the story in pairs or groups first. Go over the story orally with the whole class and help the children to write key vocabulary on the board.

Remind the children that stories are usually written in the past tense.

Ask the children to write their stories, then check them in pairs. Go over their answers with the class and check them individually. Discuss any common mistakes with the class, and discuss individual mistakes with individual children.

WB4 PAGE 3

4

Ask the children to work in pairs to arrange the pictures in order and tell the story. Go over the answers with the class.

Ask the class to find mistakes in Azim's story. Discuss them with the children: *What should Azim have written?* Ask the children to work in pairs to underline the mistakes and write out the correct version of the story.

Check and discuss with the class, writing the story out correctly on the board.

Answer:

A visit to my aunt
Yesterday I went to my aunt's house. I arrived at two o'clock. My aunt gave me a glass of orange juice. Then I helped my aunt and my uncle in the yard. I cut some grass and I saw a snake. It was long and black. My uncle wanted to kill the snake but the snake escaped through a hole in the fence.

Extra activities and teaching aids

1 · Stories exhibition

Ask the children to draw a scene from a favourite story and write about it. Ask individual children to talk about their stories to the class. Display the drawings on the classroom wall, perhaps arranged in categories, e.g. stories about magic; animal stories.

2 Storytelling

Follow up exercise 3 in the Pupils' Book by helping the children to write their story. They could also draw pictures and/or do role plays based on the story.

3 Completing a story

The children could work in pairs or groups to complete the story in Exercise 2 of the Workbook.

4 Stories about objects

Bring things to class, e.g. an old shoe, a key, a broken cup, for the children to create stories around. Ask questions: *Who do you think this shoe belonged to? Was it an old person or a young person?* Ask them to find out what they can by looking at the object, then to imagine things that happened to it and tell its story.

5 Dictation

Dictate the beginning of a story for the children to write. (Dictate first at normal speed for speech, then slowly for them to write, finally at normal speed for them to check what they have written.)

One day / Ken went home from school / and switched on the radio. / He heard a very strange / story on the news. / A man had found / some huge footprints / in his garden . . .

The children could complete the story orally or in writing.

6 Spelling check

Test the spellings of words that the children have had difficulty with in their stories.

OBJECTIVES OF THIS UNIT
- to develop the children's awareness of the history of place names
- to read and understand a passage about history
- to develop the children's ability to use proper names of countries
- to discuss different languages spoken by the class
- to develop the children's ability to use adjectives describing nationality
- to develop the children's ability to write about a place

Language skill area	Teaching/learning strategies	Where found
Speaking and lsitening	Discussing a reading passage	PB1
	Discussing languages	PB3, WB2, Ac2
	Discussing the history of their country	PB6, Ac4
	Dictation	Ac5
Grammar	Using nationality adjectives: *She is French.*	PB4, WB3, Ac3
Reading	Reading a passage about place names	PB page 5
	Answering questions about the passage	PB1, WB1
	Reading and answering questions about a graph	WB2
	Reading greetings in other languages	PB7
Spelling	Plurals of words ending in '-y'	PB5, WB5, WB6, WB7
	Spelling check	Ac6
Writing	Writing answers to questions	PB2
	Writing about languages	PB3
	Writing about countries	WB4, Ac1
	Writing about nationalities	WB4, Ac3
	Writing a guided composition	PB6
	Writing from dictation	Ac5

KEY (All references relate to sections in this unit of the Teacher's Guide)

PB2	=	Activity 2 of Unit 2 in *Pupils' Book 4*
WB3	=	Activity 3 of Unit 2 in *Workbook 4*
Ac1	=	Activity 1 in the *Activities and teaching aids* section of this unit

Using the Pupils' Book

PB4 PAGE 5 Discuss the names of places in the Caribbean with the class. Ask: *Who was Christopher Columbus? Where did his ships sail from? What language did Christopher Columbus and his men speak?*

Discuss the meanings of some key words from the reading passage: *to settle, warrior, explorer, peak, to rule, independence.*

Ask the children to read the passage on Pupils' Book page 5 on their own.

PB4 PAGE 6

1

Read and discuss the questions with the class. Ask supplementary questions: *What did the Arawak people do? Were the Caribs different from the Arawaks?* Ask the children to find the sentences in the reading passage which give the answers to the questions.

Ask the children about places they know: *Do you know any other Spanish place names? How did our (town) get its name?* etc.

2

Ask the children to write their answers in their books as full sentences, then to read and check them, working in pairs. Go over the answers again orally with the class before correcting the children's writing.

3

Ask about the language(s) the children speak at home. Count the number of children who speak each language, and help them to make a sentence, as in the example.

PB4 PAGE 7

4

Read about adjectives with the class and ask questions: *What do adjectives tell us? Can you think of some examples of adjectives?* Revise adjectives and write samples on the board. Ask the children to tell you adjectives that can describe people, e.g. *young, old, tall, clever, pretty.* Read the list of countries and adjectives.

Ask the children to work in pairs to complete the sentences. Check the answers orally with the class, then ask the children to write the sentences in their books.

Answers: a) Spanish, b) French, c) British, d) Grenadian.

5

Read the spelling rule with the class and explain vowels and consonants. Give the children examples to change on the board: *story, city, country, fairy, baby, lady.* Contrast these with such words as *donkey, monkey, day, toy.*

PB4 PAGE 8

6

Read and discuss the questions with the class. Help the class to imagine the landscape of their area before human settlement. Ask them to list the things that are there now which wouldn't have been there before. If possible, take the children outside to look around them. Elicit things that have been introduced; buildings, roads, crops, etc. Help them to find out about trees and plants that were imported from elsewhere. Then elicit things that there could have been more of, e.g. trees, flowers, birds and animals.

Ask the children to draw pictures of how they imagine things looked before the arrival of people. (This will help them with their descriptions.) Ask the children to talk about their pictures in groups. Discuss the pictures with the class.

Ask the children to write their stories in their story books, following the instructions in this exercise.

Discuss how to check the stories with the class, then ask the children to check their stories in pairs or groups.

Read the stories with the class.

7

Read the greetings aloud with the class.

Note: Ciao (Italian) means Hello and Goodbye; Bonjour (French) means Hello; Guten Tag (German) means Hello; Buenos Dias means Hello in Spanish; Au revoir (French) means Goodbye; Auf Wiedersehen (German) means Goodbye; Adios (Spanish) means Goodbye; Sayonara (Japanese) means Goodbye.

Using the Workbook

WB4 PAGE 4 **1**

Ask the children to do the exercise alone or in pairs after reading the passage on page 5 of the Pupils' Book.

Answers: Xaymaca – Jamaica; La Trinidad – Trinidad; Domingo – Dominica; Las Nievas – Nevis; Hayti – Haiti; Tobaco – Tobago.

2

Look at the graph with the class and answer the first question together. Ask the children to work on their own or in pairs to answer the other questions. Check and discuss the answers with the class.

WB4 PAGE 5 **3**

Ask the children to work in pairs to complete the table. Check the answers with the class.

Answers: American, Jamaican, French, Spanish, Danish, Mexican, Trinidadian.

4

Do the first example with the class, then ask the children to continue on their own. Check the answers with the class.

Answers: b) She comes from Holland. c) They come from Spain. d) They come from Guyana. e) They come from Canada. f) She comes from Barbados.

WB4 PAGE 6 **5**

Do the first example with the class, then ask the children to complete the table on their own. Check the answers with the class.

Answers: cities, dairies, diaries, parties, babies, countries, factories, stories, families, bodies.

6

Ask the children to read and complete the spelling rule box, working in pairs. Check the answers with the class.

Answers: To make nouns plural that end in a vowel plus 'y', you add 's'.

day – days

To make nouns plural that end in a consonant + y, you change the 'y' into 'i' and add 'es'.

story – stories, diary – diaries, city – cities.

7

Do the first example together, then ask the children to write the other sentences in pairs. Check the answers with the class.

Answers: a) I picked a lot of lilies. b) The donkeys ate all the grass. c) We played with some puppies. d) Some boys came to our house.

Extra activities and teaching aids

1 Make an old map

Ask the children to trace or draw a map of the Caribbean with the old names of the islands written in. They could colour and illustrate their maps with old ships, etc. and 'age' their maps by painting them with cold coffee or tea.

2 Language graph

The children could make a graph like the one in Exercise 2 of the Workbook to show which languages are spoken at home by the children in their class.

3 Nationalities

Collect with the children magazine pictures of famous people from different countries. Help the children to make a collage and write captions: *This is … . She is American.*

4 Stories from history

If possible, find out and read to the children accounts written by early visitors to their country or show them pictures showing how things looked in the past.

5 Dictation

The stories that we tell / in the Caribbean / come from countries / all over the world.

6 Spelling check

Test the spellings of words that the children have had difficulty with in their compositions.

OBJECTIVES OF THIS UNIT
- to read and understand a story from history
- to develop the children's ability to recognise and use the past tense
- to develop the children's ability to imagine and write about the past
- to plan and describe a time capsule
- to develop the children's ability to write a composition

Language skill area	Teaching/learning strategies	Where found
Speaking and listening	Discussing a reading passage	PB1, WB1
	Talking about life in the past	PB3, Ac2
	Talking about a time capsule	PB7 ,Ac3
	Role play based on the story	Ac1
	Dictation	Ac4
Grammar	Using the simple past tense: *The Arawaks ate parrots.*	PB4, WB2, WB3, WB4
Reading	Reading a story about history	PB page 9
	Answering questions about the passage	PB1, WB1
	Reading for information	Ac2
Spelling	Vowel digraph 'ea'	PB5, WB5
	Spelling check	Ac5
Writing	Writing answers to questions	PB2, WB1
	Writing sentences in the past tense	PB3, WB3
	Writing about life in the past	PB6, WB1
	Writing about a time capsule	PB7
	Describing an event from different points of view	PB6
	Writing from dictation	Ac4

KEY (All references relate to sections in this unit of the Teacher's Guide)
PB2   =   Activity 2 of Unit 3 in *Pupils' Book 4*
WB3   =   Activity 3 of Unit 3 in *Workbook 4*
Ac1   =   Activity 1 in the *Activities and teaching aids* section of this unit

Using the Pupils' Book

PB4 PAGE 9
Look at the illustration of the story and discuss it with the class. Ask them to say what they already know about the Arawaks and the Caribs: *Where did they live? What were they like?*

Ask the children to read the passage, then tell what new facts they have learned about the Arawaks and the Caribs.

PB4 PAGE 10
1
Ask the children to read the questions and choose the correct answers.

Read the questions with the whole class and discuss the answers, e.g. *Where does it say in the passage that the Arawaks were peaceful? What's the word that means the opposite of peaceful? Can you think of an animal that is fierce?* etc.

Answers: a) 2, b) 3, c) 1, d) 2, e) 2, f) 3, g) 2, h) 3, i) 3.

2
Ask the children to write the correct answers in their books, as sentences. Do some examples on the board, e.g. a) *There are a hundred years in a century.* b) *The Arawaks were peaceful people.*

3
Read the passage again with the class, then read and discuss the questions in this exercise one by one.

Simplify each question by breaking it up to elicit answers, e.g. *What kind of people were the Arawaks? What were the Spaniards like? Did they look very different from the Arawaks? How did they feel about the Spaniards?* Encourage the children to think about the questions and use their powers of deduction to predict what the outcome was likely to be. Discuss the questions very thoroughly and try to get all the children in the class to express an opinion.

When you are sure that the children have some ideas about what might have happened, ask them, working in pairs or groups, to write three sentences about what happened next. They could also draw pictures showing what they thought happened. Ask the children to read their sentences aloud to the class.

PB4 PAGE 11
4
Read the Remember box and the examples of the past tense with the class. Ask questions: *What is a verb? When do we use the past tense of verbs? Look at the reading passage. Can you find some examples of verbs in the past tense? Can you find an example of a verb that ends in '-ed'? Do all past tense verbs end in '-ed'? Can you find any past tense verbs in the passage that don't end in '-ed'?*

Ask the children to think of sentences in the past tense about things that happened yesterday. Write some examples on the board and underline the verbs.

Look at the sentences with the class and ask: *Why do we use the past tense when we speak and write about the Arawaks?* Do the first example with the class, then ask the children to complete the other examples on their own.

Check the answers with the class.

5
Read the words in the box aloud with the class. Ask: *What sound do all the words have?* Then ask the class to complete the sentences, using the words in the box. Check the answers with the class.

Answers: a) bread, b) feathers, c) spread, d) heads, e) dead, heaven.

PB4 PAGE 12
6
Read the introduction and the questions with the class. Ask the children to work in groups to discuss the answers to the questions. Ask them to think about the

things that the Arawaks found surprising about Christopher Columbus's men. Ask them if there would be things that they did not understand about them. What were they?

Go from group to group, listening to their discussions, and prompting them with questions if necessary.

Go over the questions with the whole class, asking each group what they think. Make notes for the Arawaks' description of the strangers and the sailor's description of the Arawaks on the board.

Then ask the children to write their descriptions in their books. Discuss first the tense they think they should use for their descriptions.

Ask the children to read and check their descriptions, working in pairs or groups. Then ask individuals to read aloud to the class.

When you evaluate the children's writing, check that they are factually correct, and that the children have included all the details they know about.

7

Read about the time capsule with the class. Ask the children to discuss in groups what they would like to bury in their time capsule. Discuss their answers with the whole class. Ask the children to explain their choices.

Then ask the children to write about their choices: *I will put in ... to show ...*

Ask the children to read what they have written to the class.

Using the Workbook

WB4 PAGE 7

1

The children could do this exercise on their own after reading the passage in the Pupils' Book, either in class or for homework. Read and discuss the children's answers with the class.

Answers: *The Arawaks:* a) They had stone weapons. b) They had brown skins. c) They used small canoes.
The Spaniards: a) They had iron weapons. b) They had white and pink faces. c) They used large sailing ships.

WB4 PAGE 8

2

After reading about the past tense in the Pupils' Book, ask the children to do this exercise, working on their own or in pairs.

Read and discuss the answers with the class.

Answers:
The *present* tense and the past *tense*.

We use the *past tense* to talk and write about things that happened in the past and which are finished.

Example: Peter *played* with his friends yesterday.

3

Point out that these things happened yesterday, so must be written about in the past tense. Explain that Peter did the same things yesterday as he does every day.

This exercise can be done in class or for homework. Check the answers orally with the class.

Answers: a) Peter got up early yesterday. b) He ate cornflakes for breakfast. c) He caught the bus to school. d) He worked hard at school. e) Peter and his friends played after school. f) He helped his mother.

WB4 PAGE 9

4

Ask the children to do this exercise on their own (it could be homework), then check their answers in pairs. Check the answers with the class, and ask children to make sentences about the Arawaks etc., using the past tense verbs.

Answers: believed, brought, caught, came, decorated, ate, faced, fell, feared, flattened, gathered, grew, happened, had, kissed, lifted, lived, made, saw, slept.

5

The children could do this exercise in pairs. Check the answers orally with the class.

Answers: 1 bread, 2 dead, 3 leather, 4 heavy, 5 head, 6 lead.

Extra activities and teaching aids

1 Role play

The children could role play the first meeting between the Arawaks and the Spaniards.

2 Research project

The children could find out more about the Arawaks, the Caribs, and/or Christopher Columbus and report back to the class.

3 Time capsule display

Groups of children could draw and label the things they would put in a time capsule, or more ambitiously, collect and label real items and display them in the classroom. They could then role play historians of the future unpacking and explaining each item in the time capsule.

4 Dictation

Dictate the following passage for the children to write. (Dictate first at the speed of normal speech, then slowly for them to write, finally at normal speed for them to check what they have written.)

In 1492 / three sailing ships arrived / and some sailors came ashore. / The sailors wore armour / and had iron weapons.

5 Spelling check

Check the spelling of words that the children have found difficult.

OBJECTIVES OF THIS UNIT
* to develop the children's ability to read for information
* to teach the children to make nouns from verbs
* to develop the children's ability to talk about feelings
* to develop the children's ability to write about feelings
* to develop the children's awareness of songs and music

Language skill area	Teaching/learning strategies	Where found
Speaking and listening	Discussing a reading passage	PB1, WB1
	Talking about feelings	PB3
	Talking about jobs	Ac2, Ac4
	Singing a song	PB7
	Dictation	Ac5
Grammar	Nouns from verbs: *A person who works is a worker.*	PB4, WB2, WB3, Ac2, Ac3, Ac4
	Using the past tense	PB5
Reading	Reading a passage about slavery	PB page 13
	Reading true/false statements about the passage	PB1
	Putting sentences from the passage in order	WB1
	Reading about music	PB7
Spelling	Past tense verbs with *ought*	PB5
	Nouns from verbs ending in '-er'	PB4, WB2
	Spelling check	Ac6
Writing	Writing sentences about the passage	PB2
	Writing sentences with nouns from verbs	PB4, WB2, Ac3
	Writing a story	PB6
	Writing a guided composition	WB4, WB5

KEY	**(All references relate to sections in this unit of the Teacher's Guide)**	
PB2	=	Activity 2 of Unit 4 in *Pupils' Book 4*
WB3	=	Activity 3 of Unit 4 in *Workbook 4*
Ac1	=	Activity 1 in the *Activities and teaching aids* section of this unit

Using the Pupils' Book

PB4 PAGE 13

Read the words of the song with the class. Discuss its meaning.

Ask the children about Emancipation Day: *When is it? What does it celebrate?* etc. Discuss the key words: *freedom, grave, plantation, pass a law, celebrate.*

Ask the children to read the passage on page 13 on their own.

PB4 PAGE 14

1

Read and discuss the statements with the class. Ask the children to say whether the statements are true or false. Ask the children to find the sentences in the reading passage which give the answers to the questions.

Answers: a) true, b) false, c) false, d) false, e) true, f) false, g) false, h) true, i) true.

2

Ask the children to write their answers in their books as full sentences, then read and check them in pairs. Go over the answers again orally with the class before correcting the children's writing.

3

Read the instructions and discuss slavery with the class. Read the adjectives and ask the children to say which ones describe the way the slaves felt. Ask the children to explain why the slaves felt like that. Ask them to think of things the slaves could not do and what the freed slaves could do after Emancipation.

PB4 PAGE 15

4

Read the first **Remember** box with the class. Ask: *Can you tell me some nouns? Is 'boy' a person, a place or a thing? Can you tell me a noun that always has a capital letter?*

Make the first noun (*farmer*) with the class then ask the children to work on

their own or in pairs to make the other examples and write them in their books. Check the answers with the class.

Now read the second **Remember** box, and ask the children to write the sentences.

Check the answers with the class.

5

Read the past tense verbs with the class. Ask: *When do we use the past tense? Can you find any past tense verbs in the reading passage? Why are the verbs in the passage in the past tense?*

Ask the children to complete the sentences, working in pairs, then check them with the class.

PB4 PAGE 16

6

Read and discuss the instructions with the class. Ask the children to imagine a slave's life, eliciting words to describe what they have to do and words to describe their feelings. Write key words on the board. Discuss which things they would miss and what they would do as soon as they were set free.

Ask the children to write their compositions in rough, then discuss them in pairs or groups. Check individual children's work.

Ask the children to write out their compositions in their books.

7

Read and discuss the instructions with the class. Sing the song with the class.

Using the Workbook

WB4 PAGE 10

1

Ask the children, working in pairs or on their own, to do this exercise after reading the passage on page 13 of the Pupils' Book. Read and check the answers with the class.

Answers: 5, 7, 1, 3, 6, 4, 2.
Ask the children to discuss the pictures in pairs then write about them. Check the answers with the class.

WB4 PAGE 11

2

Do the first example with the class, then ask the children, working in pairs, to complete the other sentences. Check the answers with the class.
  Ask the children if they can think of any other examples of similar words.

Answers: a) It is a pencil sharpener. b) It is a tin opener. c) It is a windscreen wiper. d) It is a cassette player. e) It is a grass cutter. f) It is an egg beater.

3

Ask the children to read and complete the rules, working in pairs or groups. Check and discuss the answers with the class.

Answers: *mix* becomes *mixer; wipe* becomes *wiper; cut* becomes *cutter; dig* becomes *digger.*

WB4 PAGE 12

4

Ask the children to read the adjectives in the box and write them in the spaces, working on their own or in pairs. Go over the answers with the class.

Answers: *Good feelings:* happy, pleased, glad, cheerful, delighted, content; *Bad feelings:* sad, sorrowful, angry, miserable, hurt, displeased.

5

Do the first example with the class, eliciting as many different answers as possible. Then ask the children to write the other sentences on their own. Children read and discuss their answers in pairs or groups. Then read and discuss the answers with the class.

Extra activities and teaching aids

1 History project

Help the children to find out how the slaves lived in their country. Collect pictures for the children to look at and copy. The children could act out scenes from history, e.g. slaves talking about their lives, slaves receiving the news of their emancipation.

2 Music – playing

Ask any children who can play a musical instrument to bring it to class and play for the other children.

3 Singing

Write the melody line of some well-known songs on the board for the children to follow the notes and sing together.

4 Guessing games

Ask children to think of a job (or a tool) for the rest of the class to guess by asking questions: *Do you work outside? Do you sell things to people?* etc.

5 Dictation

The settlers bought the slaves/ to work for them. / The slaves were miserable / because they wanted their freedom.

6 Spelling check

Test the spellings of words that the children have had difficulty with in their compositions.

OBJECTIVES OF THIS UNIT
- to enable the children to read, understand and appreciate a poem
- to develop the children's ability to imagine and write conversations
- to teach children the use of contractions
- to encourage the children to observe, speak and write about birds

Language skill area	Teaching/learning strategies	Where found
Speaking and listening	Discussing a reading passage	PB1
	Making up a conversation	PB3, Ac4
	Talking about birds	PB5, WB1, Ac1
	Dictation	Ac5
Grammar	Using contractions: *It's far too small*	PB4, WB4, Ac3, Ac4
Reading	Reading a poem	PB page 17
	Answering questions about the poem	PB1
	Reading instructions	PB5
	Reading about birds	WB1, WB2, WB4
	Reading for information about Belize	Ac2
Spelling	Spelling check	Ac6
Writing	Writing answers to questions	PB2
	Writing a dialogue	PB3, Ac4
	Using contractions in sentences	PB4, WB3, Ac3
	Writing facts about birds	PB5, WB5, Ac1

KEY (All references relate to sections in this unit of the Teacher's Guide)		
PB2	=	Activity 2 of Unit 5 in *Pupils' Book 4*
WB3	=	Activity 3 of Unit 5 in *Workbook 4*
Ac1	=	Activity 1 in the *Activities and teaching aids* section of this unit

Using the Pupils' Book

PB4 PAGE 17

Discuss birds with the class. Ask the children to think of as many different birds as they can. Ask them why people keep birds in cages. Read aloud to the class the poem on page 17 of the Pupils' Book. Then ask the children to read the poem on their own. Invite individual children to read the poem, in whole or in part, aloud on their own.

PB4 PAGE 18

1

Read and discuss the questions with the class. Ask the children to find the sentences which give the answers to the questions.

2

Ask the children to write their answers in their books as full sentences, then read and check them, working in pairs. Go over the answers again orally with the class before correcting the children's writing.

3

Discuss how the parrot felt in the poem. Ask the children to imagine how animals in cages might feel. Read the sample conversation with the class, then ask the children to suggest other things the tigers might say to each other.

Ask the children to work in pairs to make up a conversation and write it out in their books. Ask them to read their conversations aloud to the class and discuss what they say.

PB4 PAGE 19

4

Read about the short forms with the class. Ask the children to read them aloud and make full sentences, e.g. *I'm a girl. You're sitting near the window.*

Read the dialogue with the class. Ask the children to make the short forms orally. Then ask them, working in pairs or groups, to write the dialogue in their books with short forms.

Check and discuss the answers with the class, writing the short forms on the board. The children can read the conversation aloud in pairs.

PB4 PAGE 20

5

Read the instructions for the project with the class. The children can work in pairs or groups to make their lists of birds. If possible, provide a reference book for the children to check the names of the birds they see.

The children can also work in groups to find out more about their chosen birds, then present their findings to the class, showing their pictures and talking about the birds.

6

Ask the children to find and colour Belize on the map on pages 61-62 in the Workbook.

Using the Workbook

WB4 PAGE 13

1

Ask the children to work in pairs to read the words and label the picture. Check the answers with the class.

2

Ask the children to read and match, then check their answers in pairs.

WB4 PAGE 14

3

Ask the children to use short forms to write the conversation in the speech bubbles. Check the answers with the class. Ask the children to read the conversation in pairs.

Answers: 2 It's time for lunch. / You're wrong. It isn't. / 3 She's late. / No, she isn't. 4 She's coming now. / I can't see her.

UNIT 5

WB4 PAGE 15

4

Ask the children to work in pairs to read the descriptions and match them with the birds in the pictures. Ask them to write the answers in their workbooks. Check the answers with the class.

Answers: a) It is a hummingbird. b) It is a pelican. c) It is a scarlet ibis.

5

Then ask the children, working in pairs, to write a similar description of the other bird in the pictures. The bird that is not matched is a keskidee. You can tell the children its name before they describe it, or you can use the picture on the front of the Pupils' Book to help them guess its name.

Read and discuss their answers with the class.

Extra activities and teaching aids

1 Poster

The children could work in groups to design posters to persuade people to look after the yellow-headed parrots.

2 Belize project

The children could find out more about Belize to make a wall display or part of the scrapbook.

3 Strip cartoons

The children can work in groups to draw and write (using short forms) strip cartoons to display on the classroom wall.

4 Zoo conversations

Ask the children to imagine that they can magically talk to the animals in a zoo and imagine the conversations. They could write these down and act them out.

5 Dictation

There aren't many / yellow-headed parrots left. / It's unkind / to keep wild birds in cages.

6 Spelling check

Test the spellings of words that the children have had difficulty with in their projects.

OBJECTIVES OF THIS UNIT
- to encourage the children to discuss a topic (bush medicine)
- to develop their reading skills
- to practise describing symptoms and ailments
- to practise the use of verbs
- to teach the children how to recognise the subject of a sentence

Language skill area	Teaching/learning strategies	Where found
Speaking and listening	Discussing a reading passage	PB1
	Talking about a person	PB5, Ac1
	Talking about bush medicines	Ac2
	Role play: a visit to a doctor	PB6
	Dictation	Ac5
Grammar	Recognising verbs and subjects	PB4, WB2, Ac4
Reading	Reading a passage about a person	PB page 21
	Reading about bush medicines	PB page 21
	Reading about ailments	PB6, WB3, Ac3
	Answering questions about the passage	PB1
Spelling	'ch' pronounced 'k'	WB1
	Spelling check	Ac6
Writing	Writing answers to questions	PB2
	Using the present simple tense in sentences	PB3
	Writing sentences about symptoms and ailments	WB3, Ac 2, Ac 3
	Putting missing verbs in sentences	PB4
	Writing a description of a person	PB5, Ac1
	Writing a story	WB4

KEY (All references relate to sections in this unit of the Teacher's Guide)

PB2	=	Activity 2 of Unit 5 in *Pupils' Book 4*
WB3	=	Activity 3 of Unit 5 in *Workbook 4*
Ac1	=	Activity 1 in the *Activities and teaching aids* section of this unit

Using the Pupils' Book

PB4 PAGE 21

Discuss grandparents. Ask: *What can your grandparents do? Do they tell you stories? Do they work hard? Do you like to visit them? Why?* Discuss illnesses. Ask: *Have you ever been ill? What did you have? How did you feel? Who looked after you?*

Introduce and explain the following key words from the story: *standpipe, measles, chicken pox, mumps, sprain, cure, birth, death.*

Ask the children to read the story on page 21 of the Pupils' Book on their own.

PB4 PAGE 22

1

Read and discuss the questions with the class. Ask supplementary questions to help the children to understand the story. Ask the children to find the sentences in the reading passage which give the answers to the questions.

2

Ask the children to write their answers in their books as full sentences, then read and check them in pairs. Go over the answers again orally with the class before correcting the children's writing.

3

Revise verbs with the class. Ask the children to say what a verb is (elicit a 'doing word'). Find examples of things that Mama Dot does in the passage, then ask the children to continue, working in pairs. Check and discuss answers with the class, then ask the children to write the sentences in their books.

PB4 PAGE 23

4

Read about verbs with the class. Explain that the sentences **a-e** have verbs missing. Do the first example with the class, asking the children to suggest the missing verb. Then ask the children to continue the exercise in pairs. Check and discuss the answers with the class.

Answers: a) Mama Dot only sleeps for a few hours. b) She goes to the standpipe for water. c) She says what the weather will be. d) The children are sometimes ill. e) Mama Dot is never ill.

Read about subjects with the class. Do the first example (a) with the class, then ask the children to do the other examples in pairs. Check and discuss the answers with the class.

Grammar note:
The subject can be more than one word; make sure that the children understand this, e.g. *Her cures / The children.*

Answers: a) <u>Mama Dot</u> bakes bread. b) <u>She</u> prepares medicine. c) <u>Her cures</u> always work. d) <u>The children</u> obey Mama Dot. e) <u>She</u> knows many things. f) <u>Her grandchildren</u> love her.

Read the joke with the class. Then ask pairs of children to say the joke aloud, or to tell other doctor jokes that they know.

PB4 PAGE 24

5

Read and discuss the questions with the class.

Ask the children to each draw a picture of their special person, then talk about that person, in pairs or groups. This will help them to focus their ideas on the subject.

Read and discuss the outline of the composition with the class. Do a sample composition on the board, either the whole composition or key phrases/sentences.

Ask the children to write their compositions in their story books, then read and check their compositions in pairs.

Read selected compositions with the class.

6

Read the dialogue aloud with the class, then ask the children to practise it in pairs. Read the symptoms with the class, then ask the children, in pairs, to make up similar dialogues, taking it in turns to be the doctor and the patient. Ask pairs of children to demonstrate their dialogues to the class.

Using the Workbook

WB4 PAGE 16

1

Read the instructions and do the first example with the class. Ask the children to work in pairs to find the other examples. Check and discuss the answers with the class.

Answers: ache, Christmas, chemist, stomach, orchestra.

2

Do this exercise after Exercise 4 in the Pupils' Book, pointing out the differences between singular (*was*) and the plural (*were*) forms of the verbs. Do the first example with the class, then ask the children to continue in pairs. Check and discuss the answers with the class.

Answers: a) *The sun* was rising. b) *A bird* was flying over the house. c) *A dog* barked. d) *Some children* were playing outside the house. e) *A man* drove past the house.

WB4 PAGE 17

3

Read about Jamal with the class, then do the next example orally with the class. Ask the children to write about the other children, working on their own or in pairs. Check and discuss the answers with the class.

Answers:

b) Miranda went to see the doctor because she had a cough and a sore throat. The doctor said that she had influenza.

c) Andy went to see the doctor because he had a sore throat and he could not swallow. The doctor said that he had tonsillitis.

d) Ruth went to see the doctor because she had a runny nose and blisters on her body. The doctor said that she had chicken pox.

WB4 PAGE 18

4

Ask the children to tell the story orally, working in pairs or groups. Then tell the story with the class, writing key words on the board.

The children write their stories in their workbooks, then read and check them in pairs or groups. Check and discuss the stories with the class.

Extra activities and teaching aids

1 Mama Dot

The children could make posters (drawings or collages) in groups, showing all the things that Mama Dot does.

2 Bush medicines

The children could find out about other bush medicines and make a scrapbook or a poster with recipes and illustrations. They could also bring plants, etc. to class to look at.

3 Medicines

Discuss with children the dangers of leaving medicines lying around. Get them to make posters warning people to follow the instructions carefully: *Keep medicines away from babies and young children,* etc. Read the instructions on medicine bottles with the children.

4 Missing verbs

Give the children more examples of sentences with missing verbs (as in Pupils' Book Exercise 4) written on the board for practice.

5 Dictation

*Mama Dot treated her friend / because
she had a headache. / She gave her friend
some special medicine.*

6 Spelling check

Test the spellings of words that the
children have had difficulty with in their
compositions.

OBJECTIVES OF THIS UNIT
- to practise talking and writing about family relationships
- to enable the children to read and understand a passage about family history
- to develop the children's ability to use apostrophe 's' for possession
- to teach them to recognise and understand a prefix

Language skill area	Teaching/learning strategies	Where found
Speaking and listening	Discussing a reading passage	PB1
	Talking about family history	PB3, PB6, PB7, Ac3
	Talking about the past	Ac1, Ac2
	Dictation	Ac5
Grammar	Using apostrophe 's' for ownership: *My father's mother*	PB4, WB1
Reading	Reading about family histories	PB page 25
	Answering questions about the passage	PB1
	Reading about St. Lucia	Ac4
Spelling	Prefixes: 'dis'	PB5, WB2
	Spelling check	Ac6
Writing	Writing answers to questions	PB2, WB3
	Writing family history	PB6
	Drawing and labelling a family tree	PB7, Ac3
	Writing a composition about the past	WB4, Ac1, Ac2

KEY (All references relate to sections in this unit of the Teacher's Guide)

PB2	=	Activity 2 of Unit 7 in *Pupils' Book 4*
WB3	=	Activity 3 of Unit 7 in *Workbook 4*
Ac1	=	Activity 1 in the *Activities and teaching aids* section of this unit

Using the Pupils' Book

PB4 PAGE 25

Read and discuss the introduction to the story and the illustration with the class. Ask the children to read the story on page 25 of the Pupils' Book on their own.

PB4 PAGE 26

1

Read and discuss the questions with the class. Ask the children to find the sentences in the reading passage which give the answers to the questions.

Answers: a) 2, b) 1, c) 2, d) 2, e) 2, f) 2.

2

Ask the children to write their answers in their books as full sentences, then read and check them in pairs. Go over the answers again orally with the class before correcting the children's writing.

3

Read and discuss the questions with the class.

PB4 PAGE 27

4

Grammar note: Stress that apostrophe 's' is used for ownership here. Use examples in the classroom e.g. *Kwesi's book. Melissa's pencil case.* There is a danger that the children will use apostrophes when they are not required if they do not completely understand how they are used.

Read about and discuss apostrophe 's' with the class. Read the example with the class, then ask the children to complete the other sentences working in pairs. Check and discuss the answers with the class.

Answers: b) My uncle is my *mother's brother* or my *father's brother.* c) My grandparents are my *parents'* parents. d) My great-aunt is my *grandmother's sister* or my *grandfather's sister.*

5

Read and discuss the explanation with the class. Explain that prefixes are groups of letters that go on the front of other words to change the meanings. Read the example with the class, then ask the children to change the other sentences in the same way. Go over the answers together.

Answers: b) My friend disagreed with me, as she had checked the facts. c) It is not always a good idea to distrust everyone you meet. d) You must not always think that everyone is dishonest about everything. e) He held out his hand and the ring disappeared as if by magic.

PB4 PAGE 28

6

Read and discuss the instructions with the class. Ask: *Who is the oldest person in your family? Where does he/she live? Was he/she born there?* Help the children by finding out local details, e.g *Many people came to live here when (the factory opened). Did anybody in your family come here then? Where did they come from?*

7

Do an example of a family tree on the board. Ask questions about it: *Who is ...'s uncle? What relation is ... to ...?* Ask the children to draw their own family trees and talk about them in pairs or groups.

8

Read the instructions with the class and ask the children to find and colour St. Lucia on the map on pages 61-62 of their Workbook.

Using the Workbook

WB4 PAGE 19

1

Read the instructions and do the first example with the class. Ask the children to write the other sentences and check their answers in pairs. Check and discuss the answers with the class.

Answers: 1 This is John's bag. 2 These are his sisters' bags. 3 These are his mother's shoes. 4 This is his grandmother's umbrella.

2

Read the example with the class, then ask the children to write the other sentences in their books. Read and check the answers with the class.

Answers: b) She disagrees with her sister. c) He is displeased with his work.

WB4 PAGE 20

3

Look at the family tree and the first example with the class. Ask the children to answer the other questions in pairs, then check and discuss them with the class.

Answers: 2 Philip is Gary's father. 3 Sarah is Alicia's mother. 4 Lisa is Ellen's mother. 5 Philip's children's names are Gary and Ellen. 6 Mary is Ellen's grandmother.

WB4 PAGE 21

4

Look at the picture with the class, and help the children to make sentences about what people used to do. Write key words on the board. Then ask the children to complete and write the sentences in their Workbooks. Read aloud and check their answers with the class.

Extra activities and teaching aids

1 Project – Life in the past

Ask the children to find out about life in their area in the (recent) past, contrasted with life now, e.g. find out about newish buildings, roads, airports, etc. and what people did before they were built. They could choose a topic to work on in groups, e.g. clothes, transport, shopping, work.

2 Interview about the past

Arrange for the children to interview an older local person about life in their area in the past. Ask the children to prepare some questions to ask before the interview. Ask them questions about what they found out after the interview, then ask them to write about what they found out.

3 Family tree

The children could make and talk about the family tree of a favourite fictional character (from a book, film or TV), adding extra imaginary characters to the family tree.

4 St. Lucia project

The children could find out more about St. Lucia and make a poster.

5 Dictation

My grandmother / is my mother's mother / or my father's mother. / My mother and father / are my parents.

6 Spelling check

Test the spellings of words for members of the family.

Assessment 1

PB4 PAGE 29 To assess the children's abilities fully, these exercises should be done with minimal guidance from the teacher. The children should also work on their own.

Check the children's work and record their performance using a chart similar to the one illustrated on page 13.

Grade the children for factually correct answers, correct use of the main grammar points, punctuation of the sentences, spelling and handwriting.

Answers

1 This exercise is about correcting mistakes in writing.
My favourite stories are about Sprat Morrison. Sprat is a Jamaican boy and he is always getting into trouble. He saves an old woman's life in a bush fire.

2 This exercise tests the use of adjectives for nationality.
   b) Sir Garfield Sobers is a famous Barbadian cricketer.
   c) Derek Walcott is a famous St. Lucian writer.
   d) Louise Bennet is a famous Jamaican poet.
   e) Clive Lloyd is a famous Guyanese cricketer.
   f) V.S. Naipaul is a famous Trinidadian writer.

3 (languages)
a) French b) English c) Spanish d) Chinese

PB4 PAGE 30 4 This exercise tests the past tense of verbs.
arrived; grew; ate; caught; refused; thought; wore; slept; fought

5 This exercise concerns the vowel combination 'ea' in spelling certain words.
b) w<u>ea</u>ther c) d<u>ea</u>ths d) spr<u>ea</u>d e) r<u>ea</u>d

6 This exercise is about nouns formed from verbs.
   b) A person who drives is a driver.
   c) A person who runs is a runner.
   d) A person who bowls is a bowler.
   e) A person who swims is a swimmer.
   f) A person who wins is a winner.

PB4 PAGE 31 7 This exercise concerns the short forms of verbs.
it's; isn't; I'm; You'll; we're; Don't; don't

8 This exercise concerns the subjects of sentences.

<u>A goldfinch</u> returned to her nest one day and found it empty. <u>Someone</u> had taken her children. All day <u>she</u> searched for the baby birds. In the evening <u>the goldfinch</u> found her children in a cage by a window. <u>They</u> were cheeping for her to let them out. For hours <u>the poor mother bird</u> tried to peck open the cage door, but in vain. The next day <u>the goldfinch</u> returned to her children. Very slowly and sadly <u>she</u> fed them through the bars of the cage. One by one <u>the little birds</u> died. <u>The mother bird</u> had given them poisonous herbs. To the goldfinch <u>death</u> seemed better than the loss of freedom.

9 This exercise tests the ability to correct mistakes.
Leonardo da Vinci wrote this fable of the goldfinch and her babies.
Leonardo was a famous Italian writer, scientist and painter who lived in Italy in the 16th century.

PB4 PAGE 32 10 This exercise tests the correct use of apostrophe 's' for ownership.
Who is my parents' fathers' grandchild's mother?
Answer: Your mother.

11 This exercise tests the correct use of
apostrophe 's' for ownership.
*The Caribs were fierce fighters. They
bound their babies' heads between two
boards to lengthen and strengthen
their skulls. Often the Spaniards'
swords broke on Carib fighters' heads.
One of the Caribs' favourite weapons
was the butu. This was a club with
sharp stones fixed in it.*

12 This exercise tests the use of the prefix
'dis' to denote opposites.
  b) The girl was <u>dis</u>honest and we
     <u>dis</u>trusted her.
  c) I <u>dis</u>liked the taste of the
     medicine.
  d) After drinking it, the pain
     <u>dis</u>appeared.
  e) The doctor was <u>dis</u>pleased with
     the results.

OBJECTIVES OF THIS UNIT
- to develop the children's ability to predict outcomes
- to enable children to read and understand a traditional story
- to teach the use of personal pronouns
- to develop their ability to write a story

Language skill area	Teaching/learning strategies	Where found
Speaking and listening	Discussing a reading passage	PB1
	Predicting the outcome of a story	PB3
	Telling a story	PB5, WB3
	Role play based on the story	Ac2
	Dictation	Ac5
Grammar	Using pronouns: *She gave him her comb.*	PB4, WB1, WB2
Reading	Reading a folktale	PB page 33
	Answering questions about the story	PB1
Spelling	Opposites of adjectives	WB5
	Spelling check	Ac6
Writing	Writing answers to questions	PB2
	Writing a possible ending to a story	PB3
	Using pronouns in sentences	PB4
	Writing a folk story	PB5, WB4, Ac1
	Describing a picture	WB6

KEY (All references relate to sections in this unit of the Teacher's Guide)

PB2	=	Activity 2 of Unit 8 in *Pupils' Book 4*
WB3	=	Activity 3 of Unit 8 in *Workbook 4*
Ac1	=	Activity 1 in the *Activities and teaching aids* section of this unit

Using the Pupils' Book

PB4 PAGE 33

Read and discuss the introduction to the story with the class. Explain the following words from the story: *lure, wicker, go mad, wrinkled.*

Ask the children to read the passage on page 33 of the Pupils' Book on their own.

PB4 PAGE 34

1

Read and discuss the questions with the class. Ask the children to find the sentences in the reading passage which give the answers to the questions. Ask the children to retell the story in their own words.

2

Ask the children to write their answers in their books as full sentences, then read and check them in pairs. Go over the answers again orally with the class before correcting the children's writing.

3

Read and discuss the questions with the class. Encourage the children to answer as fully as possible. Ask the children to write their own endings to the story, then read them in pairs or groups. The children could also draw pictures to go with the stories.

PB4 PAGE 35

4

Read about pronouns with the class and ask questions: *Can you find a pronoun in the story? Can you find any more pronouns?* Help the children to make their own sentences with pronouns, e.g. *Kwesi is sitting near the window. Melissa is sitting next to him. Ruth is sitting in front of her.*

Do the first sentence in the passage with the class. Ask the children to work in pairs or groups to read the rest of the passage and replace the nouns with pronouns orally. Go over the answers with

the class, then ask the children to write out the passage in their books.

Answer: Jon-Jon was a rich man and *he* lived in a big house.

Ma Bec lived with Jon-Jon but nobody knew why *she* was there. Jon-Jon saw a fairmaid. *She* gave *him* her comb. The fairmaid asked *him* to go and live with *her. She* gave *him* some pearls. *He* found *them* in his basket.

PB4 PAGE 36

5

Read and discuss the instructions with the class. Ask the children to draw their pictures and tell their stories in groups. Then ask them to write the story in their story book.

6

The children find and colour Guyana on their maps on pages 61-62 of their Workbook.

7

The children find and colour Grenada on their maps on pages 61-62 of their Workbook.

Using the Workbook

WB4 PAGE 22

1

Read and discuss the instructions, then do the first example with the class. Ask the children to do the other sentences on their own or in pairs. Check and discuss the answers with the class.

Answers:

a) *Jamal* likes going to the beach with his friends.
   He likes going to the beach with his friends.

b) *His friends* often go there with Jamal and his sister.
   They often go there with Jamal and his sister.

c) _His sister_ has found a beautiful shell.
She has found a beautiful shell.

2

Do the first sentence orally with the class,
then ask the children, on their own or in
pairs to write the sentences in their
Workbooks. Check and discuss the
answers with the class.

Answers: a) Jamal is looking for it. b) His
friends are helping him. c) A crab is
approaching her.

WB4 PAGE 23

3

Ask the children to tell the story, working
in pairs or groups. Tell the story again
with the class, writing key words on the
board.

4

Read and discuss the time expressions
with the class. Then help the children to
make a sentence orally about each of the
pictures, using the time expressions. Ask
the children to write the sentences in
their Workbooks, then read and check the
answers in pairs.

WB4 PAGE 24

5

Explain the instructions to the class, then
ask the children to complete the
crossword puzzle, checking their answers
in pairs. Check and discuss the answers
with the class.

Answers: _Down:_ 1 black, 3 wet, 4 shiny,
6 full, 8 deep
Across: 2 ugly, 3 wise, 5 richest, 7 young,
9 late.

6

Read and discuss the words in the box
with the class. Ask the children to work
in pairs to make sentences, following the
example. Check and discuss the answers
with the class.

Extra activities and teaching aids

1 Pictures from the story

The children could draw pictures
illustrating the story and write about
them. They could make a collage showing
the fairmaid, using silver paper to show
her glistening tail.

2 Role play from the story

Ask the children to act out scenes from
the story.

3 Fishing

Ask the children to name, describe and
draw the different kinds of fish they can
buy in the market.

4 Shiny things

The children could make a classroom
display with pictures or real objects that
are shiny.

5 Dictation

_The fairmaid / put some pearls / in Jon-
Jon's basket. / She asked him / to go and
live with her._

6 Spelling check

Test the spellings of words that the
children have had difficulty with in their
stories.

OBJECTIVES OF THIS UNIT
- to develop the children's ability to read and talk about a folktale
- to teach the use of reflexive pronouns
- to develop their ability to write a description of a precious possession
- to widen their vocabulary

Language skill area	Teaching/learning strategies	Where found
Speaking and listening	Discussing a reading passage	PB1, WB1
	Pronunciation of '-ask-' words	PB3
	Acting a play	Ac1
	Discussing precious possessions	Ac3
	Dictation	Ac5
Grammar	Using reflexive pronouns: *The fairmaid looked at herself.*	PB4, WB3, WB4
Reading	Reading a folktale	PB page 37
	Answering questions about the passage	PB1, WB1, WB2
Spelling	Plural of words ending in 'f'	PB5, WB5
	Spelling check	Ac6
Writing	Writing answers to questions	PB2
	Writing a play	Ac 1
	Using reflexive pronouns in sentences	WB4, Ac2
	Writing a description of a precious possession	PB6, Ac4

KEY (All references relate to sections in this unit of the Teacher's Guide)		
PB2	=	Activity 2 of Unit 7 in *Pupils' Book 4*
WB3	=	Activity 3 of Unit 7 in *Workbook 4*
Ac1	=	Activity 1 in the *Activities and teaching aids* section of this unit

Using the Pupils' Book

PB4 PAGE 37
Discuss the story so far with the class. Ask the children to re-tell the story and revise their predictions for what will happen next.

Ask the children to read the passage on page 37 of the Pupils' Book on their own.

PB4 PAGE 38

1
Read and discuss the questions with the class. Ask the children to find the sentences in the reading passage which give the answers to the questions.

Answers: a) 3, b) 2, c) 2, d) 1, e) 2, f) 2.

Ask the children to retell the story in their own words.

2
Ask the children to write their answers in their books as full sentences, then read and check them in pairs. Go over the answers again orally with the class before correcting the children's writing.

3
Read the sentences aloud with the class. Invite individual children to read. Ask the children, working in pairs, to practise reading the sentences, checking each other's pronunciation of '-ask'.

PB4 PAGE 39

4
Read about the reflexive pronouns with the class. Help the children to make their own sentences with the pronouns. Ask questions: *Did you enjoy yourself yesterday? Have you ever cut yourself? What do you do when you hurt yourself?*

Do the first sentence with the class, then ask the children to work on their own or in pairs to complete the other sentences. Check and discuss the answers with the class.

Answers: a) herself, b) himself, c) myself, d) yourself, e) themselves, f) ourselves, g) yourselves.

5
Read and discuss the spelling rule with the class. Ask the children to look at the pictures in pairs and make sentences orally (*knife/knives, leaf/leaves, calf/calves, wolf/wolves*). Check the answers with the class, then ask the children to write the sentences in their exercise books.

PB4 PAGE 40

6
Read and discuss the questions and the instructions with the class. Ask the children to discuss the questions in pairs or groups.

Write (or make notes for) a sample composition on the board, then ask the children to draw and write about their most precious possessions in their story books.

Invite individual children to read their compositions to the class.

7
Read and discuss the instructions with the class. Ask the children to suggest things that could go in the basket. Then ask the children to draw and write in their books, discussing in groups or pairs where the things come from.

Go over the answers orally with the class, writing difficult words and sentences on the board.

Using the Workbook

WB4 PAGE 25

1
Read the instructions with the class and revise subjects. Do the first sentence together, then ask the children, on their own or in pairs, to complete the remaining sentences. Read and check the answers with the class.

Answers: a) Ma Bec, b) Jon-Jon, c) The fairmaid, d) Jon-Jon, e) The fairmaid, f) Ma Bec.

2

This exercise is also based on the story. Read the instructions and the example with the class. Ask the children to work in pairs to rewrite the rest of the sentences in the same way. Read and discuss the answers with the class.

Answers: b) the fairmaid, c) the fairmaid, d) the basket, e) Ma Bec.

WB4 PAGE 26

3

Look at the table with the class and do some of the answers orally. Then ask the children to write in the missing words and check their answers in pairs. Check and discuss the answers with the class (write the completed table on the board).

Answers: yourself, himself, herself, itself, ourselves, yourselves, themselves

4

Ask the children to use pronouns from the table in the previous exercise to complete the postcard. Do the first example orally with the class, then ask the children to complete the rest of the postcard in pairs. Read the answers with the class.

Answer:

We are enjoying *ourselves* in Tobago. We went shopping and I bought *myself* a T-shirt. Daddy bought *himself* a hat and Mummy got *herself* some sandals. We saw some pelicans catching fish for *themselves* in the sea. Hope you are all enjoying *yourselves*.

WB4 PAGE 27

5

Do the first example with the class. Ask the children to continue, working on their own or in pairs. Read and discuss the answers with the class.

Answers: a) The shelves are opposite the window. b) The thieves stole Mr Green's vegetables. c) The farmer is proud of his new calves. d) She put some

handkerchieves in her bag. e) Aunt Rosa took the knives out of the drawer. f) Jamal bought some loaves of bread for his mother. g) The fishermen told me about their lives.

6

Look at the chart with the class and make sentences about it orally. Ask the children to write the sentences, then check them in pairs. Check and discuss the answers with the class.

Extra activities and teaching aids

1 Write a play

Ask the children, working in groups to write a play based on the story *The Fairmaid of Karika*. Divide the play into scenes and ask different groups to write different parts of the story. Ask the children to practise and perform their play.

2 Writing a postcard

The class could draw and write their own postcards, based on the one on page 26 of the Workbook.

3 Guessing game

Ask the children to think of their most precious possessions for the rest of the class to guess by asking questions: *Is it big or small? Do you keep it at home? Do you use it every day?* etc.

4 Autobiographies of things

Ask the children to think of a precious object, e.g. a pearl, and write its life story.

5 Dictation

The thieves stole the pearls / from a box on the shelf. / Then they ran away / and hid themselves / among the leaves.

6 Spelling check

Test the spellings of words the children have had difficulty with in their compositions.

OBJECTIVES OF THIS UNIT
- to develop the children's ability to read for information
- to enable the children to discuss a topic and express an opinion
- to teach the use of collective nouns
- to develop the children's ability to write a report of an event

---

Language skill area	Teaching/learning strategies	Where found
Speaking and listening	Discussing a reading passage	PB1
	Talking about manatees	PB3, Ac2
	Telling a story	PB5, WB5
	Role play: an interview	Ac4
	Dictation	Ac6
Grammar	Using collective nouns: *A swarm of bees.*	PB4, WB3, WB4, Ac3
	Using prepositions: *She was on a rock.*	WB2
Reading	Reading a passage about manatees	PB page 41
	Answering questions about the passage	PB1, WB1
	Reading about Martinique	Ac5
Spelling	Spelling check	Ac7
Writing	Writing answers to questions	PB2
	Writing sentences	WB1
	Writing a report of an incident	PB5, WB5
	Writing about manatees	Ac2
	Writing imaginary diaries	Ac1

KEY (All references relate to sections in this unit of the Teacher's Guide)

PB2	=	Activity 2 of Unit 10 in *Pupils' Book 4*
WB3	=	Activity 3 of Unit 10 in *Workbook 4*
Ac1	=	Activity 1 in the *Activities and teaching aids* section of this unit

Using the Pupils' Book

PB4 PAGE 41 Discuss the picture and the diary entry with the class, then ask the children to read the passage on page 41 of the Pupils' Book on their own.

PB4 PAGE 42 **1**
Read and discuss the statements with the class. Ask the children to find the sentences in the reading passage which tell them whether the statements are true or false. Ask further questions about the passage to make sure that the children have understood it.

Answers: a) false, b) true, c) true, d) false, e) true, f) true, g) true, h) false, i) false, j) true.

2
Ask the children to write the sentences, then read and check them in pairs. Go over the sentences again orally with the class before correcting the children's writing.

3
Read and discuss the questions about manatees with the class. Encourage them to form their own opinions and to give reasons for them.

PB4 PAGE 43 **4**
Read about and discuss collective nouns with the class. Ask questions: *What kinds of animals go around in groups? What do we call a group of ...?* Elicit further collective nouns, e.g. *band, flock.*
Do the first read-and-match example with the class. Then ask the children to work in pairs to match the collective nouns with the animals. Check and discuss the answers with the class, then ask the children to write the collective nouns in their exercise books.

PB4 PAGE 44 **5**
Read and discuss the instructions with the class. Ask the children to suggest sentences for the different parts of the story and write key words and phrases on the board. Ask the children to write their reports in their story books. They should make their reports look like newspaper reports with a headline and a picture.

Note: If you can find and read with the class suitable newspaper stories from the local press, this will give the children a better idea of the way newspaper reports are put together.
Ask the children to read their reports in pairs or groups. Ask children to read their reports aloud to the class.

6
Ask the children to find and colour Martinique on the map on pages 61-62 of their Workbook.

Using the Workbook

WB4 PAGE 28 **1**
Do the first sentence orally with the class, then ask the children to write the other sentences, on their own or in pairs. Read and discuss the answers with the class. Ask the children to make their own sentences with the same pattern.

Answers: a) The manatee is a mammal which eats water plants. b) Speedboats are boats which travel very fast. c) Chemicals are substances which pollute the sea. d) Mermaids are creatures which have tails like fish. e) Martinique is an island which is in the Caribbean.

2
Read the prepositions in the box with the class and do the first example with the class. Then ask the children on their own or in pairs to write the prepositions in the gaps. Read and discuss the answers with the class.

Answer: There is a large rock *off* the south coast of the island. The distance *from* the rock to the coast is three kilometres. Some of the sailors thought that they saw a mermaid sitting *on* the rock. They say that she jumped *in* the sea. They watched her swimming *near* the rock *for* ten minutes. This mermaid was seen *by* six members of the crew.

WB4 PAGE 29 **3**

Fill in the first gap with the class and then ask the children to fill in the rest of the rule, working in pairs. Check the answers with the class.

Answers: A collective *noun* is the name of a *collection* of people or things.
   We say: A *team* of players.

4

Ask the children to match the collective nouns and then write the expressions. Check the answers with the class.

WB4 PAGE 30 **5**

Ask the children to tell the story orally in pairs or groups. Then ask them to tell it as a class. Write difficult words or expressions on the board.
   On their own or in pairs, the children write the story in their Workbooks. Read and discuss the children's stories with the class.

Extra activities and teaching aids

1 Diaries

Ask the children to write sailors' diaries, like the one on page 41 of the Pupils' Book, telling about the strange things they have seen on their travels. Read the diaries with the class.

2 Manatee poster

The children, in groups, could think of ways to help the manatees, and make a poster telling people what they could do to save them.

3 Collective nouns game

The first player says "I went for a walk yesterday and I saw a flock of sheep." The next adds something else to the list, for example: "I went for a walk yesterday and I saw a flock of sheep and a swarm of bees." The game continues like this around the class.

4 Manatee role plays

The children could role play the reporter's interviews for the newspaper story in Exercise 5 of the Pupils' Book.

5 Martinique project

The children could do a project to find out more about Martinique and make a poster or a scrapbook.

6 Dictation

When we were swimming yesterday / we saw a herd of manatees. / Some of them were basking on the rocks.

7 Spelling check

Test the spellings of words that the children have had difficulty with in their compositions.

OBJECTIVES OF THIS UNIT
- to develop the children's ability to read fiction
- to encourage them to discuss the topic (bullying at school) and form their own opinions
- to widen their vocabulary and enable them to use alternatives to overused adjectives
- to enable the children to write about their personal experiences

Language skill area	Teaching/learning strategies	Where found
Speaking and listening	Discussing a reading passage	PB1
	Discussing bullying at school	PB3, PB6
	Talking about life at school	Ac1
	Role play: bullying	Ac2
	Dictation	Ac5
Grammar	Using alternative adjectives	PB4, WB3, WB4
Reading	Reading a story	PB page 45, WB5
	Answering questions about the passage	PB1, WB1
	Reading about Jamaica	Ac4
Spelling	Soft 'c' before 'i', 'y' and 'e'	PB5, WB2
	Spelling check	Ac6
Writing	Writing answers to questions	PB2
	Using words with soft 'c' in sentences	PB5
	Writing about an experience	PB6, WB5

KEY (All references relate to sections in this unit of the Teacher's Guide)

PB2 = Activity 2 of Unit 11 in *Pupils' Book 4*

WB3 = Activity 3 of Unit 11 in *Workbook 4*

Ac1 = Activity 1 in the *Activities and teaching aids* section of this unit

Using the Pupils' Book

PB4 PAGE 45 Discuss the picture and read the introduction with the class. Before reading, discuss the meanings of the following words and expressions: *ring leader, encourage, take kindly to.*

Ask the children to read the passage on page 45 of the Pupils' Book on their own.

PB4 PAGE 46 **1**

Read and discuss the multiple-choice statements with the class. Ask the children to find the sentences in the reading passage which give the answers to the questions.

Answers: a) 2, b) 1, c) 2, d) 2, e) 1, f) 2, g) 1.

2

Ask the children to write their answers in their books as full sentences, then read and check them in pairs. Go over the answers again orally with the class before correcting the children's writing.

3

Discuss the questions with the class. Ask: *How do you think you would feel if you had to go to a new school?* If any of the children in the class are recent arrivals, invite them to describe their feelings. Discuss bullying, and ask: *How do you think you would feel if someone was bullying you? Is it wrong to bully other children?* etc.

PB4 PAGE 47 **4**

Read about and discuss overused adjectives with the class. Ask the children to suggest things that can be described as nice or as nasty.

Read the paragraph with the class and ask the children to find the words *nice* and *nasty*. Ask the children to say what these words describe, e.g. Hope's English clothes. Ask the children to work in pairs to find words to replaces *nice* and *nasty*.

Check and discuss the answers orally with the class. Ask the children to write the paragraph with the new words in their exercise books.

Read the answers again with the class.

5

Read the words aloud with the class. Read and discuss the **Remember** box. Ask the children to suggest other words that have the same sound, e.g. *ceiling, bicycle, recent, circus.*

Ask the children, working in pairs, to find the correct words to complete the sentences. Check the answers with the class.

Answers: a) certain, b) recent, c) decent, d) lucky.

PB4 PAGE 48 **6**

Read and discuss the questions with the class. Ask the children to discuss the questions in pairs or groups, then write their compositions in their storybooks.

Finish with a discussion of bullying with the class. Ask the children what they should do to stop bullying.

7

Ask the children to find and colour Jamaica on the map on pages 61-62 of their Workbook.

Using the Workbook

WB4 PAGE 31 **1**

Ask the children to do the crossword puzzle after reading the story on page 45 of the Pupils' Book. Ask them to check their answers in pairs, before checking with the whole class.

Answers: *Down:* 1 Kingston; *Across:* 2 skipping, 3 shriek, 4 alone, 5 group, 6 English, 7 city, 8 tongue, 9 uniform.

2

Ask the children to read the words aloud in pairs and find the words with the /s/ sound. Check the answers with the class.

Answers: spicy, century, celebrate, receive, cement, ceiling.

WB4 PAGE 32

3

Ask the children to say what kind of words these are (elicit 'adjectives'.) Ask them to draw lines to join the pairs of adjectives, then discuss their answers in pairs. Check the answers with the class, and ask the pupils to make sentences with the words.

Answers: nice/nasty; friendly/unfriendly; new/old; kind/unkind; pleasant/unpleasant; clean/dirty; smiling/frowning; soft/loud; polite/rude.

4

Read and discuss the instructions with the class, and do the first sentence with the class. Ask the children to complete the rest of the paragraph working on their own or in pairs. Read and discuss the answers with the class.

Answer: Now Lester is a friendly boy. He is kind to animals and pleasant to all the people he meets. His face is always smiling and his voice is polite and soft. He usually wears a clean, new cap.

WB4 PAGE 33

5

Discuss the picture with the class, then read the instructions together. Ask the children to work out the correct order of the sentences on their own or in pairs. Read and check the answers with the class. Ask the children to suggest ways of completing the story, and discuss these with the class. Then ask the children to write an ending to the story, on their own or in pairs.

Read and discuss the endings with the class.

Answers: 2, 1, 5, 7, 3, 6, 8, 4.

Extra activities and teaching aids

1 Comparing schools

The children can compare the school in the reading passage with their own school. Ask them first to say what they can find out about the school in the story, e.g. *the girls like skipping; the school is in the country*. Then ask them how the school in the story is different from their own school.

2 Bullying role play

After discussing bullying, ask the children to role play a situation in which someone is bullied, and show how the situation can be remedied.

3 Matching pairs

Write pairs of adjectives + opposites on small pieces of paper and card and distribute them around the class. The children read the word aloud and find their partner. (This activity can be used for choosing random partners for pairwork.)

4 Jamaica project

The children can do a project to find out more about Jamaica.

5 Dictation

When Hope started her new school / she did not have the proper uniform. / The other girls bullied her / because she came from a city school. / Her teacher advised her / to dress like the other girls in the class.

6 Spelling check

Test the spellings of words that the children have had difficulty with in their compositions.

OBJECTIVES OF THIS UNIT
- to develop the children's ability to read fiction
- to teach the use of proper nouns
- to encourage the children to discuss a topic and form their own opinions
- to develop the children's ability to write a description of a place

Language skill area	Teaching/learning strategies	Where found
Speaking and listening	Discussing a reading passage Talking about leaving home Describing a place Dictation	PB1 PB3, PB7 PB6, Ac 3, Ac4 Ac5
Grammar	Using proper nouns Using pronouns	PB4, WB3, Ac1, Ac2 WB4
Reading	Reading a story Answering questions about the passage	PB page 49 PB1, WB1
Spelling	Words ending in '-ure' Spelling check	PB5, WB2 Ac6
Writing	Writing answers to questions Writing a description of a place Using proper nouns in sentences Writing about favourite things	PB2 PB6 PB4 WB5

KEY (All references relate to sections in this unit of the Teacher's Guide)

PB2 = Activity 2 of Unit 12 in *Pupils' Book 4*

WB3 = Activity 3 of Unit 12 in *Workbook 4*

Ac1 = Activity 1 in the *Activities and teaching aids* section of this unit

Using the Pupils' Book

PB4 PAGE 49 Discuss the story from Unit 11 with the class the read the introduction to the story on page 49 of the Pupils' Book and look at the picture together.

Before reading, discuss the meanings of the following words and expressions: *I doubt it; tend to; a born … .*

Ask the children to read the passage on page 49 the Pupils' Book on their own.

PB4 PAGE 50

1

Read and discuss the questions with the class. Ask the children to find the sentences in the reading passage which give the answers to the questions. Ask the children to discuss the story in their own words.

2

Ask the children to write their answers in their books as full sentences, then read and check them in pairs. Go over the answers again orally with the class before correcting the children's writing.

3

Discuss the questions with the class. Ask: *Would you like to live in another country? Where would you like to go? Why?*

PB4 PAGE 51

4

Read about proper nouns with the class and ask questions: *Can you tell me a proper noun? What other kinds of words are proper nouns? What is special about the way we write proper nouns?* Elicit the names of people and places that the children know.

Ask the children to read the passage in pairs and find the proper nouns. Read the passage with the class, checking and discussing the answers. Ask the children to copy the passage giving the proper nouns capital letters.

Answer: On Friday, Hope's last day before leaving for England, she and her brother, Joshua and her sister, Ruth, went round the farm saying goodbye to all the animals. Joshua refused to part with his kitten, Jemima. His grandfather had to prise her away and give her to Aunt Esme who was staying in Jamaica.

5

Read the words with the class. Ask the children to complete the sentences on their own or in pairs.

Answers: a) adventure, b) picture, c) future, d) nature, e) furniture.

PB4 PAGE 52

6

Read and discuss the instructions with the class. To focus their thoughts, the children could draw pictures of their favourite places and talk about these in groups before they write.

The children write their compositions in their storybooks. Check and discuss in the usual way.

7

Read the instructions with the class. Ask: *What do you notice about this list?* (The things are in alphabetical order.)

Using the Workbook

WB4 PAGE 34

1

Read the instructions and do the first example with the class. Ask the children to complete the sentences, working in pairs. Check and discuss the answers with the class.

Answers: a) describe, b) feelings/thoughts, c) thought, d) amazement, e) announce, f) reflect.

2

Do this exercise after doing Exercise 5 in the Pupils' Book. Ask the children to work in pairs to write the names of the books, e.g. to include *future* or *nature*. Check the answers with the class.

WB4 PAGE 35

3

Ask the children, working in pairs, to find the six proper nouns and complete the sentences. Do the first example with the class. Check and discuss the answers with the class.

Answers: a) France is a country in Europe. b) Saturday, c) August, d) Barbados, e) David.

4

Revise pronouns with the class. Ask: *Can you tell me a pronoun? Can you find any pronouns in the story in the Pupils' Book? Can you make a sentence using a pronoun? What's the pronoun in your sentence?*

Fill the first gap in the exercise with the class. Then ask the pupils to complete the paragraph, working on their own or in pairs. Check and discuss the answers with the class.

Answer: Alicia put her books away. Then <u>she</u> and Peter went into the kitchen to help their mother. <u>They</u> both peeled the vegetables and put <u>them</u> in a pot to cook. Peter put some food in a bucket and took <u>it</u> outside to feed the chickens. As soon as <u>they</u> heard <u>him</u>, the chickens came running.

WB4 PAGE 36

5

Read and discuss the instructions and do the first example together. Ask the children to continue, working in pairs. Read and discuss the answers with the whole class. (This exercise can be used to prepare for the composition – Exercise 6 in the Pupils' Book.)

Extra activities and teaching aids

1 Finding proper nouns

Give the children small sections cut from a newspaper and ask them to underline the proper nouns.

2 Proper nouns Buzz

As a variation of the counting game Buzz, ask the children to read a passage aloud, each child reading a sentence, and substituting the word "Buzz" for each proper noun. Go back to the beginning when a child makes a mistake.

3 *Our favourite places* display

Make a display with drawings (or photos) of the children's favourite places. Relate them (with flags?) to a map of the area where the children live.

4 Guess the place

One child thinks of a place and the others have to guess where it is by asking questions (*Is it near here? Is it a town?* etc.)

5 Dictation

Hope did not want / to leave Jamaica at first. / She did not want / to go to England / in an aeroplane.

6 Spelling check

Test the spellings of words that the children have had difficulty with in their compositions and the words ending in '-ure'.

OBJECTIVES OF THIS UNIT
- to deevlop the children's ability to read and understand a poem
- to encourage them to discuss the topic (describing the weather – snow and rainstorms)
- to teach the use of adverbs of manner
- to develop the children's ability to write a poem

Language skill area	Teaching/learning strategies	Where found
Speaking and listening	Discussing a poem	PB1, PB3
	Describing a tropical rainstorm	PB3
	Talking about the weather	Ac 2, Ac4
	Telling a story	WB6
	Dictation	Ac5
Grammar	Using adverbs of manner: *The snow fell silently*	PB4, WB3, WB4. WB5, Ac3, Ac4
Reading	Reading a poem	PB page 53
	Answering questions about the poem	PB1
	Reading about snow	PB7
Spelling	Rhyming words	PB5
	Adverbs ending in '-fully'	WB3, WB4, WB5
	Spelling check	Ac6
Writing	Writing answers to questions	PB2
	Using similes in sentences	WB1, WB2, Ac2
	Writing sentences with adverbs	Ac3
	Writing a poem	PB6, Ac1
	Writing a story	WB6

KEY (All references relate to sections in this unit of the Teacher's Guide)

PB2	=	Activity 2 of Unit 13 in *Pupils' Book 4*
WB3	=	Activity 3 of Unit 13 in *Workbook 4*
Ac1	=	Activity 1 in the *Activities and teaching aids* section of this unit

UNIT 13

Using the Pupils' Book

PB4 PAGE 53 Discuss the picture with the class. Ask: *Has anybody here seen snow? What do you imagine snow is like? Would you like to see snow? What would you do in the snow? What kind of clothes would you wear?* etc.

Read the poem on page 53 of the Pupils' Book aloud to the class, then ask the children to read it on their own.

PB4 PAGE 54

1

Read the poem aloud with the class.

Read and discuss the questions with the class. Ask the children to find the lines in the poem which give the answers to the questions.

2

Ask the children to write their answers in their books as full sentences, then read and check them in pairs. Go over the answers again orally with the class before correcting the children's writing.

3

Discuss the questions with the class. Write key words and phrases about a rainstorm on the board. Ask questions to elicit as full a description as possible, e.g. *What do people do when a rainstorm starts? What is the sky like? What happens to all the water?* Ask the children to write their ideas and read them in groups.

PB4 PAGE 55

4

Read about adverbs with the class. Demonstrate some adverbs in the classroom, e.g. *I'm opening the door. How am I opening it?* (Slowly); *Kwesi, can you sit down quickly? What did he do?* etc.

Read and discuss the example with the class. Ask the children, working in pairs or in groups, to use adverbs to rewrite the sentences. Check and discuss the answers with the class, then children write the sentences in their books.

Answers: b) quickly, c) slowly, d) perfectly, e) neatly.

5

Ask the children, working in pairs, to read the words aloud and find those that do not rhyme. Go over the answers orally with the class. Ask the children to find rhyming words to fit each of the lists and then to write lists of rhyming words in their books.

Answers: fume, flown, now, cone.

PB4 PAGE 56

6

Read the poem aloud and discuss it with the class. Write the word RAINSTORM vertically down the side of the board, and then ask the children to work in pairs or groups to make up their own poems. Read and discuss the children's poems with the class. The children write (and illustrate) their poems in their story books.

7

Ask the children to read this section on their own, then ask questions, e.g. *What is the amazing thing about snowflakes?*

Using the Workbook

WB4 PAGE 37

1

Read the instructions and do the first example with the class. The children write the other sentences, and then check their answers in pairs. Check and discuss the answers with the class.

Answers: a) The soap smells like flowers. b) The dog looks like a wolf. c) The juice tastes like apples. d) The girl sounds like an angel. e) The scarf feels likes a kitten.

WB4 PAGE 38

2

The children could first discuss the pictures, working in pairs or groups. Ask the children to write their answers, then read and discuss them with the class.

3

Ask the children to read about adverbs again in Exercise 4 in the Pupils' Book, then working in pairs or groups, complete the information about adverbs in the box. Check and discuss the answers with the class.

Answers:
Adverbs tell us *how* things are done. When an adjective ends in '-ful', we make it into an adverb by adding *'-ly'*. The adjective peaceful becomes *peacefully*. The adjective thankful becomes *thankfully*.

4

Read and discuss the instructions with the class. Ask the children to complete the table, then check their answers, working in pairs. Check and discuss the answers with the class.

Answers:
b) care	*careful*	*carefully*
c) *pity*	*pitiful*	pitifully
d) *regret*	regretful	*regretfully*
e) *tear*	*tearful*	tearfully

5

Read and do the first example with the class. Then ask the children to complete the paragraph working in pairs or groups. Read and discuss the answers with the class.

Answers: a) beautifully, b) careful, c) pitifully, d) regretfully, e) tears.

WB4 PAGE 39

6

Ask the children to tell the story orally in pairs or groups and think of a title for it. Tell and discuss the story with the class. Write key words and expressions on the board.

Ask the children to write the story in their Workbooks. Read and discuss the stories with the class.

Extra activities and teaching aids

1 Rainstorm poem

Ask the children to draw a picture and write a poem about a rainstorm, following the pattern of the first part of the John Agard poem.

2 A snowy day

The children could imagine that they are out in the snow and draw, talk and write about what happened.

3 Adverbs

The children, in groups, could write instructions for doing something – for example, crossing a busy street, learning to ride a bicycle – using adverbs in their instructions. Read the instructions with the class.

4 Weather

Revise weather vocabulary and combine it with adverbs, e.g. *The sun is shining brightly.*

5 Dictation

The children played / as the snow fell gently down. / The flakes landed softly / on the ground. / When the sun came out, / the snow melted / quickly.

6 Spelling check

Test the spellings of words that the children have had difficulty with in this unit.

OBJECTIVES OF THIS UNIT
- to develop the children's ability to read and understand a factual account
- to encourage them discuss a topic (ambitions) and formulate their own ideas
- to teach the correct use of prepositions
- to develop the children's ability to write a composition about a dream or ambition

Language skill area	Teaching/learning strategies	Where found
Speaking and listening	Discussing a reading passage Discussing dreams and amibitions Dictation	PB1 PB3 , PB6, Ac1 Ac5
Grammar	Using prepositions: *They sailed from Antigua to England.*	PB4, PB5, WB1, WB3, WB4, WB5, Ac2, Ac3
Reading	Reading a factual account True and false statements about the passage Reading about Antigua	PB page 57 PB1, WB1, WB2 Ac4
Spelling	Spelling check	Ac6
Writing	Writing true statements Writing a composition about dreams Writing sentences with prepositions	PB2 PB6, Ac1 PB5, WB5

KEY (All references relate to sections in this unit of the Teacher's Guide)

PB2	=	Activity 2 of Unit 14 in *Pupils' Book 4*
WB3	=	Activity 3 of Unit 14 in *Workbook 4*
Ac1	=	Activity 1 in the *Activities and teaching aids* section of this unit

Using the Pupils' Book

PB4 PAGE 57 Discuss the picture and read the introduction with the class. Use a map to get the children to show where Harold La Borde's yacht went. Before reading, discuss the meanings of the following words and expressions: *ashore, hot water bottle, climate, bombard, sacrifice, security, obviously, haunt.*

Ask the children to read the passage on page 57 of the Pupils' Book on their own.

PB4 PAGE 58

1

Read and discuss the statements with the class. Ask the children to find the sentences in the reading passage which give the answers. Ask further questions to make sure that the children have understood the passage. Read the passage aloud with the class.

Answers: a) true, b) true, c) false, d) false, e) true, f) true, g) true, h) false, i) true, j) true.

2

Ask the children to write the true statements in their books as full sentences, and then – working in pairs – to read and check them. Go over the answers again orally with the class before correcting the children's writing.

3

Discuss the questions with the class. The children could draw pictures to illustrate their ambitions and talk about them in groups.

PB4 PAGE 59

4

Read about prepositions with the class. Ask the children to make sentences using prepositions: *Can you make a sentence using 'on' about something in the room?* (*My book is on the desk.*)

5

Read the instructions with the class. Ask the children, working in pairs, to fit the prepositions into the gaps. Check and discuss the answers with the class. The children write the paragraphs in their books.

Answer: Harold wanted to sail *across* the Atlantic Ocean *from* Antigua *to* England. He loaded food and water *into* the boat. He put the hot-water bottle *under* the bunk bed. His wife and friend went *with* him. They stood *beside* him *on* the boat, as it set sail *towards* the open sea. The newspapermen *on* the shore waved them 'Goodbye'.

PB4 PAGE 60

6

Read and discuss the instructions with the class. Ask the children to plan their compositions and discuss sample plans with the class.

Ask the children to write and check their compositions in the usual way. Read aloud selected compositions with the class.

7

The children find and colour Antigua on the map on pages 61-62 ofthe Workbook.

Using the Workbook

WB4 PAGE 40

1

Read the instructions with the class. Ask the children to complete the sentences and check their answers in pairs. Check and discuss the answers with the class.

Answers: a) for. b) to. c) for. d) to. e) for. f) for. g) for, h) to.

2

Complete the first sentence with the class, then ask the children to do the rest of the exercise on their own or in pairs. Check and discuss the answers with the class.

Answers: f), a), c).

WB4 PAGE 41

3

Ask the children to complete the rule, working in pairs. Check and discuss the answers with the class.

4

Do the first example with the class. Then ask the children, working in pairs, to complete the other sentences. Check and discuss the answers with the class.

Answers: a) to, b) up, c) over, d) towards, e) through, f) behind.

WB4 PAGE 42

5

Do a sample drawing and sentence with the class, drawing on the board one item on the shelves and making a sentence about it.

The children draw and write on their own, then discuss and check their answers in pairs. Go over the answers with the class.

Extra activities and teaching aids

1 Our ambitions

Make a display on the classroom wall with pictures and writing about what the children want to do.

2 Preposition hunt

Give the children articles cut out of the newspaper and ask them to find and underline the prepositions in them.

3 Following instructions

Ask the children to give each other instructions, involving prepositions, e.g. *Come into the room. Go to the window. Take a book from the shelf and put it on ...,* etc.

4 Antigua project

The children find out about Antigua.

5 Dictation

Some people sailed / across the Atlantic Ocean / from Antigua to England / in a small yacht.

6 Spelling check

Test the spellings of words that the children have had difficulty with in their compositions.

Assessment 2

To assess the children's abilities fully, these exercises should be done with minimal guidance from the teacher. The children should work on their own.

Check the children's work and record their preformance using a chart similar to the one illustrated on page 13.

Grade the children for factually correct answers, correct use of the main grammar points, punctuation of the sentences, spelling and handwriting.

PB4 PAGE 61

Answers

1   This exercise tests the correct use of subject and object pronouns.
   b)   She said, "Jon-Jon, I love *you*. Come and live with *me*. *We* shall be happy together."
   c)   Jon-Jon gave the fairmaid the basket and told *her* to bale out the sea with *it*.
   d)   *They* never saw the fairmaid again. *She* never came back.
   e)   Jon-Jon loved the fairmaid's beautiful eyes. *He* still sees *them* in his dreams.

2   This exercise concerns plurals, including reflexive pronouns.
   b)   Young manatees are called calves.
   c)   The manatees cannot defend themselves against hunters.
   d)   The mermaids looked at themselves in the mirrors.
   e)   We enjoyed ourselves watching the manatees.

PB4 PAGE 62

3   This exercise concerns nouns.
   The <u>Arawaks</u> killed and ate <u>manatees</u>. The <u>Caribs</u> refused to eat <u>manatees</u> or <u>turtles</u>, because they believed it would make them slow and stupid like these <u>animals</u>. They ate <u>snakes</u>, <u>lizards</u>, <u>rabbits</u>, <u>agoutis</u> and <u>birds</u>.

4   This exercise tests the appoariate use of collective nouns.
   b)   A fleet of ships ...
   c)   A bunch of bananas ...
   d)   A shoal of fish ...
   e)   A pack of wolves ...
   f)   A herd of manatees ...

5   This exercise concerns proper nouns. The story about *Jon-Jon* and the fairmaid of *Karika* is a folktale from *Guyana*. In *Grenada* there is a lake called the *Grand Etang*. People say that a mermaid lives in the lake. Every year in *August* the people hold a feast in her honour. In *Trinidad* there are stories about a mermaid called *Mama Dlo* who guards the rivers and the seas.

PB4 PAGE 63

6   This exercise concerns the use of adjectives and their opposites.
   colourful – colourless; ripe – unripe; familiar – unfamiliar; huge – tiny; noisy – quiet; cold – hot; unfriendly – friendly.

7   This exercise concerns the use of adverbs.
   firmly, fearfully, safely.

8   This exercise concerns the use of adverbs and their opposites.
   b)   The boat's engines purred *loudly*.
   c)   The seabirds flew *noisily* overhead.
   d)   The boat sailed *quickly* and *smoothly* out of the harbour.
   e)   In England the snow fell *heavily* on the ground.
   f)   Harold's journey went *well*.

PB4 PAGE 64

9 This exercise concerns the use of
prepositions.
Harold le Borde sailed across the
Atlantic from Antigua to England in a
small yacht. When the wind was
behind the boat they travelled fast.
Sometimes gales made huge waves
that broke over the deck. Harold and
his wife stayed in their cabin below
the deck until the sea was calm again.

10 This exercise concerns the use of
prepositions.
in, on, to
along, across, about
below, beside, between
before, behind, above.

11 (soft 'c' sound)
b) centre, c) cinema, d) circle, e) cent.

OBJECTIVES OF THIS UNIT
- to encourage children to discuss the topic of food and to express their likes and dislikes
- to teach the correct use of *much* and *many*
- to teach children to make adjectives from nouns
- to widen their vocabulary by describing tastes
- to enable them to write a description of a favourite meal

Language skill area	Teaching/learning strategies	Where found
Speaking and listening	Discussing a reading passage	B1
	Describing tastes	PB3, Ac2
	Discussing food	PB6, WB6, Ac 1
	Role play: in a restaurant	Ac3
	Dictation	Ac6
Grammar	Using *much* and *many*: *We should not eat too much candy.*	PB4, WB3, WB4
Reading	Reading a passage about food	PB page 65
	Answering questions about the passage	PB1
	Adjectives in word grid	WB2
	Reading a recipe	PB7
	Reading a food diary	WB6
Spelling	Making adjectives from nouns	PB5, WB5
	Spelling check	Ac7
	Food vocabulary	WB2
Writing	Writing answers to questions	PB2
	Writing about food	WB1, WB6
	Using adjectives in sentences	PB5
	Writing a menu	PB6
	Writing a recipe	PB7, Ac 4
	Writing a food diary	Ac 5

KEY (All references relate to sections in this unit of the Teacher's Guide)

PB2	=	Activity 2 of Unit 15 in *Pupils' Book 4*
WB3	=	Activity 3 of Unit 15 in *Workbook 4*
Ac1	=	Activity 1 in the *Activities and teaching aids* section of this unit

Using the Pupils' Book

PB4 PAGE 65 Discuss the pictures of food with the class.

Ask the children to read the passage on page 65 of the Pupils' Book on their own.

PB4 PAGE 66

1

Read and discuss the questions with the class. Ask the children to find the sentences in the reading passage and the pictures which give the answers to the questions.

Answers: a)-c) children's own answers, d) ackee, yam and watermelon, e) Europe, f) roti, g) pelau, h) flying fish, i) doubles, j) children's own answer.

2

Ask the children to write their answers in their books as full sentences, then read and check them in pairs. Go over the answers again orally with the class before correcting the children's writing.

3

Discuss the questions with the class. Ask the children to think of other ways to describe food. Ask the children to draw pictures and write about their favourite and their least favourite foods: *I like/dislike ... because it tastes ... .*

Ask questions about preference: *Which do you prefer, salty food or sweet food?*

PB4 PAGE 67

4

Read about and discuss *much* and *many* with the class. Read the sample sentence and ask the children, working in pairs, to make sentences about the other foods. Check and discuss the answers with the class. The children write the sentences in their books.

Answers: b) We should not eat too many chocolate bars. c) We should not eat too much candy. d) We should not eat too much fried food. e) We should not eat too many chips. f) We should not eat too many snowcones (use the word 'ice cream' if the children are more familiar with it.).

5

Read about adjectives with the class. Ask the children to make sentences with *salty, fishy* and *peppery.*

Ask the children to make the adjectives then write sentences, working in pairs. Check and discuss the answers with the class.

Answers: spicy, icy, greasy, smoky.

PB4 PAGE 68

6

Read about and discuss the menu with the class. Help the children with the spelling of the food they like. Ask the children to draw and write out their menus and talk about them in groups. Discuss the menus with the class.

7

Read and discuss the recipe with the class. (As the recipe requires no cooking it would be possible to demonstrate and taste in the classroom.)

Discuss recipes with the class. Point out that all recipes start with a list of ingredients, and then explain how each dish is made. Ask the children to describe their own favourite food and how it is made. Discuss the different processes used in preparing food, e.g. chopping, peeling, mixing, heating, stirring, frying, baking, boiling, etc.

The children can work in pairs or groups to write their recipes. Read and discuss the recipes with the class.

UNIT 15

Using the Workbook

WB4 PAGE 43

1

Look at the map and complete the first sentence with the class. Ask the children to write the other sentences working in pairs. Check and discuss the answers with the class.

2

Ask the children to work in pairs to find the words in the square. Check the answers with the class.

Answers:

D	E	L	I	C	I	O	U	S
F	J	Y	S	H	A	R	P	W
I	V	S	P	Q	S	K	E	E
S	P	I	C	Y	A	C	P	E
H	Z	C	D	E	L	J	P	T
Y	S	K	B	I	T	T	E	R
J	O	L	G	M	Y	X	R	R
T	U	Y	T	A	S	T	Y	P
F	R	U	I	T	Y	H	O	T

WB4 PAGE 44

3

Ask the children to complete the rule. Check and discuss the answers with the class.

4

Fill the first gap with the class. Ask the children to continue on their own or in pairs. Check and discuss the answers with the class.

Answer: Sandra feels sick. She went to a party yesterday and she ate too *much* food. She did not eat *much* fruit, but she had too *many* cakes. She was thirsty and she drank too *many* sweet drinks. She did not have *much* water to drink. She also had too *many* sandwiches.

5

Do the first example with the class, then ask the children to complete the table, checking their answers in pairs. Check and discuss the answers with the class.

Answers: sugary, slimy, fruity, muddy, woolly, dusty, noisy.

WB4 PAGE 45

6

Ask the children to read the diary and find the answers to the questions, working in pairs. Check and discuss the answers with the class.

The children can write the answers in their exercise books.

Answers: a) 4, b) Wednesday, c) Tuesday, d) no, e) Tuesday, f) Monday.

Extra activities and teaching aids

1 Tasting

Bring fruit, etc. to class for the children to compare the tastes and express preferences.

2 Food comparison

The children could work in groups to compare by tasting. e.g. different kinds of snack foods or soft drinks (something that has several different varieties and is easy to divide). A group should make a table to write their results, for example as illustrated below.

Most = 4   Least = 1

	Crispness	Saltiness	Tastiness
A	3	1	2
B	4	2	4
C	1	3	1
D	2	4	3

3 Role play

Ask the children, working in groups, to write a restaurant menu, and role play a scene in a restaurant.

4 Class recipe book

Make a scrapbook with recipes, illustrated by pictures drawn by the children. Discuss quantities and measuring food, e.g. a pinch of ..., a teaspoonful of ... , ... grams of ...

Practise asking and answering questions with *How much ...* and *How many ...?*

5 Make a food diary

The children could make and discuss their own food diaries following the example in Exercise 6 in the Workbook.

6 Dictation

Sugar is made from sugarcane. / Sugar makes food taste sweet, / but you should not eat / too much sugary food.

7 Spelling check

Test the spellings of common food vocabulary.

OBJECTIVES OF THIS UNIT
- to develop the children's ability to read for information
- to encourage the children to discuss a topic (animals and their food)
- to teach the children to recognise and use homophones
- to develop their ability to write descriptions from notes

Language skill area	Teaching/learning strategies	Where found
Speaking and listening	Discussing a reading passage	PB1
	Discussing birds	PB3
	Describing an animal	PB5, Ac1, Ac3
	Dictation	Ac5
Grammar	Using punctuation in sentences	WB4
	Using possessive adjectives	WB5
Reading	Reading a factual passage	PB page 69
	Answering questions about the passage	PB1, WB1
	Playing a word game	PB6
	Reading for information about animals	Ac1
Spelling	Homophones: *hair/hare*; *sail/sale*	PB4, PB6, WB3, Ac2, Ac4
	Spelling check	Ac6
Writing	Writing answers to questions	PB2
	Writing a description from notes	PB3
	Using homophones in sentences	PB4, WB3
	Adding punctuation to a passage	WB4
	Writing a description of an animal	PB5, WB2, Ac3

KEY (All references relate to sections in this unit of the Teacher's Guide)

PB2 = Activity 2 of Unit 15 in *Pupils' Book 4*

WB3 = Activity 3 of Unit 15 in *Workbook 4*

Ac1 = Activity 1 in the *Activities and teaching aids* section of this unit

Using the Pupils' Book

PB4 PAGE 69 Discuss the picture and read the poem aloud to the class. Before reading the rest of the passage, discuss the meanings of the following words and expressions: *termite, claw, snout, sting.*

Ask the children to read the passage on page 69 of the Pupils' Book on their own.

PB4 PAGE 70 **1**

Read and discuss the questions with the class. Ask the children to find the sentences in the reading passage which give the answers to the questions. Ask the children to tell you as many facts as they can about anteaters.

2

Ask the children to write their answers in their books as full sentences, then read and check them, working in pairs. Go over the answers again orally with the class before correcting the children's writing.

3

Discuss the instructions with the class. Look at the first picture and ask the children about the different parts of a bird, e.g. feathers, wings, tail, beak. Ask them to describe the birds and to say why they have long/short legs, etc. Ask the children to discuss the birds in pairs or groups. Talk about the birds with the class and write sample sentences on the board: *The ... has a ... because it ...,* etc.

The children write about the birds in their books.

Answers: picture **a** is a pelican (fits label b); **b** is a toucan (label c); **c** is an ibis (label a).

PB4 PAGE 71 **4**

Read about and discuss homophones with the class. Do the first sample sentence with the class, then ask the children to continue, working in pairs. Check and discuss the answers with the class.

Answers: a) tail, b) their, c) Their/hairs, d) two.

Read the example of a silly sentence with the class. Read and discuss the meanings of the pairs of words. Ask the children to work in groups to draw and write other examples. Read the sentences and look at the pictures with the class.

PB4 PAGE 72 **5**

Read and discuss the instructions with the class. Try to make available reference material for the children to find out about the animals they have chosen.

The children prepare and write their compositions in the usual way, and draw their pictures on separate pieces of paper.

Display the pictures on the board or the classroom wall. Ask the children to read their compositions aloud, and ask the other children to find the pictures of the animals they are describing.

6

Read the instructions with the class. Ask the children to suggest homophones they could use, i.e. words that can be drawn.

Make a sample set of dominoes to illustrate the game and demonstrate the game for the class to see.

The children work in pairs to make their own dominoes and play the game.

Save the sets of dominoes to play later for revision.

Using the Workbook

WB4 PAGE 46 **1**

Ask the children to read the story again and find the words to match the pictures. Check and discuss the answers with the class.

Answers: 1 anteater, 2 paw, 3 anthill, 4 snout, 5 tongue.

2

Do the first example with the class, then ask the children to write the other sentences and check their answers in pairs. Check and discuss the answers with the class.

Answers: a) An anteater uses its tongue to catch termites. b) A horse uses its tail to keep flies away. c) A manatee uses its flippers to feed itself. d) A kangaroo uses its pouch to carry its babies.

WB4 PAGE 47

3

Read the instructions and do the first sentence with the class. Ask the children to work in pairs to rewrite the other sentences. Check and discuss the answers with the class.

Answers: a) heard, b) There, c) sea, d) two sails, e) red sails, f) Wait for.

4

Start rewriting the paragraph on the board with the class, then ask the children to continue, working in pairs. Check the answers by writing the rest of the paragraph on the board with the class. Ask the children to explain the punctuation: *Why do we need a full stop here?* (Because it's the end of a sentence.) etc.

Answer: Anteaters have long, sticky tongues and long snouts. They live in the forests of South America. Nowadays anteaters are in danger because hunters kill them. Sometimes their homes in the forest are destroyed and the anteaters die.

WB4 PAGE 48

5

Read the words in the box with the class and do the first sentence together. Ask the children to continue on their own, then check their answers in pairs. Check and discuss the answers with the class.

Answers: a) his, b) their, c) her, d) its, e) your, f) my.

Extra activities and teaching aids

1 Animals project

The children can find out about what different animals eat and how they are adapted. They could draw and write about the animals and tell the class what they have found out.

2 Homophones poster

The children could make a poster display to illustrate common homophones.

3 Imaginary animals

The children could invent animals adapted to eat strange diets, e.g. to account for things that go missing in a classroom (a peneater, an erasereater, say) and draw and write about these animals.

4 Recognising homophones

Write homophones on cards or on the board. Read sentences aloud, e.g. *She combed her hair.* The children have to find the right card or point to the right word, recognising it from its context.

5 Dictation

My aunt combed her hair. / Then she picked up her blue pen / because she wanted to write a letter to her son.

Ask the children to find the words in the dictation that have homophones.

6 Spelling check

Test the spellings of words that the children have had difficulty with in their compositions.

OBJECTIVES OF THIS UNIT
- to develop the children's ability to read for information
- to encourage them to discuss a topic (volcanoes)
- to teach basic syllabication
- to widen the children's vocabulary with adjectives suitable for describing volcanoes
- to develop their ability to write creatively (haikus)

Language skill area	Teaching/learning strategies	Where found
Speaking and listening	Discussing a reading passage	PB1
	Talking about volcanoes	PB3, Ac1
	Talking about a haiku	PB6
	Role play: report of an eruption	Ac4
	Dictation	Ac5
Grammar	Recognising and counting syllables	PB4, PB6
Reading	Reading a passage about volcanoes	PB page 73
	Answering multiple-choice questions	PB1, WB1, WB2, WB3
	Reading about volcanoes	Ac1
	Reading about St. Vincent	Ac2
Spelling	Consonant digraph: 'ph'	PB5, WB4
	Spelling check	Ac6
Writing	Writing answers to questions	PB2
	Writing a haiku	PB6, Ac3
	Writing a report	WB5
	Writing from dictation	Ac5

KEY (All references relate to sections in this unit of the Teacher's Guide)		
PB2	=	Activity 2 of Unit 17 in *Pupils' Book 4*
WB3	=	Activity 3 of Unit 17 in *Workbook 4*
Ac1	=	Activity 1 in the *Activities and teaching aids* section of this unit

Using the Pupils' Book

PB4 PAGE 73

Discuss the picture with the class. Ask them to say what they know about volcanoes. Before reading, discuss the meanings of the following words and expressions: *lush, deafening, molten, sulphur, lava, gas, liquid, extinct, active, fertile*.

Ask the children to read the passage on page 73 of the Pupils' Book on their own.

PB4 PAGE 74

1

Read and discuss the questions with the class. Ask the children to find the sentences in the reading passage which give the answers to the questions. Read the passage again with the class, asking questions as you read.

Answers: a) 3, b) 2, c) 1, d) 3, e) 1, f) 3.

2

Ask the children to write their answers in their books as full sentences, then read and check them, working in pairs. Go over the answers again orally with the class before correcting the children's writing.

3

Read aloud the poem on page 73 of the Pupils' Book. Discuss the questions with the class. Ask: *Why did the poet think the volcano was like a dragon?* Write the words that the children suggest on the board.

PB4 PAGE 75

4

Read about and discuss syllables with the class. Help the children to count the seventeen syllables in the haiku. Explain that the haiku is a Japanese form of poem, which can also be written in English. The words do not have to rhyme.

Ask the children to count the syllables in the words and write the answers. Check and discuss the answers with the class.

Answers: b) 2 (li-quid), c) 2 (la-va), d) 1 (rocks), e) 2 (sul-phur), f) 3 (e-rup-tion), g) 1 (ash), h) 2 (dra-gon).

5

Read the words aloud with the class. Ask the children to complete the sentences and check them in pairs. Check the answers with the class.

Answers: a) Philip b) telephone c) sulphur d) photograph e) graph

PB4 PAGE 76

6

Read the instructions with the class. Work together to compose a haiku on the board, asking the children to count out the syllables in each line, e.g.

Sinking down slowly,
Reddening the western sky,
The evening sun sets.

The children can then work in pairs or groups to write and read their own haikus. They can write and illustrate them on paper or in their story books, then read them aloud to the class.

7

The children add St. Vincent to their map on pages 61-62 of their Workbooks.

Using the Workbook

WB4 PAGE 49

1

Read the instructions and revise adjectives with the class. Ask: *Can you tell me some adjectives to describe (this pen)?* Ask the children to work in pairs to find the words that are adjectives and use them to complete the sentences.

Check and discuss the answers with the class.

Answers: a) deafening, b) lush, c) active, d) extinct, e) red-hot, f) molten.

2

Read the words with the class. Ask the children, working in pairs, to use the words to label the picture. Check and discuss the answers with the class.

WB4 PAGE 50

3

Do the first examples with the class, e.g. *Does 'twinkling' describe something you can see or something you can hear?* Ask the children to complete the lists, then read and check the answers with the class.

4

Complete the first word with the class, then ask the children to continue, working in pairs. Read and check the answers with the class.

Answers: a) photograph, b) paragraph, c) sulphur, d) apostrophe, e) elephant, f) trophy, g) dolphin, h) phantom.

WB4 PAGE 51

5

Read and discuss the instructions with the class. Ask the children to suggest sentences for the newspaper report. The children write their reports and read them in pairs or groups to check.

Read and discuss the completed reports with the class.

Extra activities and teaching aids

1 Volcanoes project

The children could find volcanoes on the map of the Caribbean and read about eruptions. They could also draw diagrams showing what happens when a volcano erupts.

2 St Vincent project

The children find out about St. Vincent.

3 Haiku scrapbook

The pupils could collect their haikus in a scrapbook.

4 Role play

The children can role play conversations between a reporter and the witnesses to a volcanic eruption.

5 Dictation

The active volcano erupted yesterday. / Smoke poured out of the volcano, / and lava flowed out of it. / The hot ash settled / on the land near the volcano.

6 Spelling check

Test the spellings of words that the children have had difficulty with in their compositions.

OBJECTIVES OF THIS UNIT
- to develop the children's reading skills
- to encourage them to appreciate and talk about art
- to widen the children's vocabulary through the use of synonyms
- to develop their ability to write stories and poems

Language skill area	Teaching/learning strategies	Where found
Speaking and listening	Discussing a reading passage	PB1
	Talking about a picture	PB3, Ac2
	Describing a place	PB6
	Dictation	Ac5
Grammar	Using synonyms in sentences	PB4, WB2, WB3, Ac3
Reading	Reading a passage about a painting	PB page 77
	Answering questions about the passage	PB1
	Reading and matching synonyms	PB4
	Reading about Trinidad	Ac7
Spelling	Silent 'c' after 's'	PB5, WB4
	Spelling check	Ac6
Writing	Writing answers to questions	PB2, WB5
	Writing a description of a place	PB6, WB1
	Comparing past and present	WB5
	Writing a poem about a picture	Ac1
	Writing a story about a picture	Ac4

KEY (All references relate to sections in this unit of the Teacher's Guide)		
PB2	=	Activity 2 of Unit 18 in *Pupils' Book 4*
WB3	=	Activity 3 of Unit 18 in *Workbook 4*
Ac1	=	Activity 1 in the *Activities and teaching aids* section of this unit

Using the Pupils' Book

PB4 PAGE 77 Discuss the picture with the class. Ask the children to describe the picture, eliciting as much detail as possible. Before reading, discuss the meanings of the following words and expressions: *traffic island, recreation, grandstand, throng, spectacle.*

Ask the children to read the passage on page 77 of the Pupils' Book on their own.

PB4 PAGE 78

1

Read and discuss the questions with the class. Ask the children to find the sentences in the reading passage which give the answers to the questions.

Exercise 2

Discuss the questions again with the class, helping them to make sentence answers. Ask the children to write their answers in their books as full sentences, then read and check them in pairs. Go over the answers again orally with the class before correcting the children's writing.

Exercise 3

Discuss the questions with the class. Elicit detailed answers and descriptions. Ask: *Do you think the artist has put his feelings into the picture? How do you think he felt about the place when he was painting it? Do you think it is easier to describe a place in a picture or in words? If you were writing a poem about this place, what would you say?*

PB4 PAGE 79

4

Note: Synonyms are not exactly interchangeable, e.g. *detest* is somewhat stronger in meaning than *hate*. The point to stress to the children here is that alternative words can be used when they are writing.

Read about and discuss synonyms with the class. Ask the children if they can think of any other synonyms.

Ask the children to read the passage in pairs and find the synonyms in the box. Check and discuss the answers with the class, then ask the children to write out the passage in their books.

Answers: wealthy/rich; schooling/education; study/learn; detested/hated; discovered/found; gift/talent; artist/painter; returned/came back; landscape/scenery; precious/valuable.

5

Note: Point out to the children that this rule only applies when ' sc' is followed by a vowel 'i 'or 'e'.

Read and discuss the spelling rule with the class. Write on the board the following sentences for the children to complete:

a) When you look at the painting you can smell the ... of the countryside.
b) Cazabon used to ride around the island and ... from his horse to make drawings of the ... .
c) Cazabon's parents wanted him to study medical ...

Ask the children to complete the sentences in their books. Check the answers with the class.

Answers: a) scent, b) descended/scenery, c) science.

PB4 PAGE 80

6

Read and discuss the instructions with the class. Ask the children to discuss and plan their compositions in pairs or groups. Discuss with the class, writing key words and expressions on the board. Discuss the different tenses the children need to use in each part of the composition.

The children write and check their compositions in the usual way.

Read some of the compositions aloud with the class.

7

The children put Trinidad on the map on pages 61-62 of their Workbooks.

Using the Workbook

WB4 PAGE 52

1

Ask the children to look at the map and find the places in the box. Fill in the first gap with the class then ask the children to continue on their own or in pairs.

Check and discuss the answers with the class.

Answers: St. Ann's River, zoo, Maraval Road, (the National Museum).

WB4 PAGE 53

2

Ask the children to complete the rule, working in pairs. Check and discuss the answers with the class.

3

Ask the children to complete the crossword in pairs. Check and discuss the answers with the class.

Answers: *Down:* miserable; *Across:* 2 remember, 3 rich, 4 close, 5 scent, 6 afraid, 7 happy, 8 valuable, 9 tale, 10 detest.

4

Ask the children to find the six words with the silent 'c' and write them in the spaces. Check the answers with the class.

Answers: scientist, scissors, ascend, scent, descent, scene.

WB4 PAGE 54

5

Ask the children to compare the two pictures, working in pairs. Discuss the answers with the class, then help them to complete the first sentence. Ask them to continue answering the questions in pairs. Check and discuss the answers with the class.

Extra activities and teaching aids

1 Haikus

The children can try writing a haiku about the picture on page 77 of the Pupils' Book.

2 Looking at paintings

Find reproductions of paintings by local or foreign artists to discuss with the children. Ask the children to choose the pictures they like best and talk or write about why they like them.

3 Synonyms

The children can make a collection of synonyms and write them in their books. They could also write the pairs of words on cards and play a matching game with them, e.g. synonym snap.

4 Stories based on pictures

Give the children pictures to tell and write stories about.

5 Dictation

The artist descended from his horse / and began to sketch the scene. / He wanted to remember all the places / that he had visited.

6 Spelling check

Test the spellings of words that the children have had difficulty with in their compositions.

7 Trinidad project

The children find out about Trinidad.

OBJECTIVES OF THIS UNIT
- to develop the children's reading skills
- to encourage the children to discuss a topic (ghosts) and to express an opinion
- to encourage them to discuss and describe emotions (fear)
- to teach the use of abstract nouns
- to develop their ability to write a story

Language skill area	Teaching/learning strategies	Where found
Speaking and listening	Discussing a reading passage	PB1
	Talking about being scared	PB3
	Telling a story	PB6, Ac2, Ac4
	Describing a picture	WB5
	Role play: ghost story	Ac1
	Dictation	Ac5
Grammar	Using abstract nouns: *They were full of fear*	PB4, WB3, WB4, Ac3
Reading	Reading a story	PB page 81
	Answering questions about the passage	PB1, WB1
Spelling	Nouns ending in '-ness'	PB5
	Spelling check	Ac6
Writing	Writing answers to questions	PB2
	Describing emotions	PB3
	Joining sentences with *but*	WB2
	Writing a ghost story	PB7
	Describing a picture	WB5
	Using abstract nouns in sentences	WB4

KEY (All references relate to sections in this unit of the Teacher's Guide)

PB2	=	Activity 2 of Unit 19 in *Pupils' Book 4*
WB3	=	Activity 3 of Unit 19 in *Workbook 4*
Ac1	=	Activity 1 in the *Activities and teaching aids* section of this unit

Using the Pupils' Book

PB4 PAGE 81 Discuss the picture with the class. Ask: *How does this picture make you feel? What do you think will happen in the story?* Before reading, discuss the meanings of the following words and expressions: *strain, crunch, panic, terror-stricken, stumble.*

Ask the children to read the passage on page 81 of the Pupils' Book on their own.

PB4 PAGE 82

1

Ask the children to read the story aloud with plenty of expression. Read and discuss the questions with the class. Ask the children to find the sentences in the reading passage which give the answers to the questions.

Note: This story comes from Antigua. The children should be able to infer what a Jack O'Lantern is from the passage.

2

Ask the children to write their answers in their books as full sentences, then read and check them in pairs. Go over the answers again orally with the class before correcting the children's writing.

3

Discuss the questions with the class. Ask the children to work in pairs or groups to list the expressions. Discuss these with the class and make a full list on the board. Ask the children to write the expressions in their books.

PB4 PAGE 83

4

Read about abstract nouns with the class. Ask the children to think of other abstract nouns and write these on the board. Ask the children to copy the passage into their exercise books. Then, working in pairs, they should circle all the nouns, and underline the abstract nouns. Check and discuss the answers with the class.

Answer: When _darkness_ falls, *people* sometimes let their _imagination_ take over. In the _blackness_, ordinary *things* can seem frightening and bring _terror_ to *people's minds.* They are full of _fear_.

5

Read the examples with the class. Ask the children to think of other words ending in '-ness'. Write these words on the board. Ask the children to write the sentences out with the words changed into nouns. Read and discuss the answers with the class.

Answers: lateness; tiredness; darkness; goodness; brightness.

PB4 PAGE 84

6

Read and discuss the instructions with the class. Ask the children to work in groups to discuss and prepare their compositions. Discuss what the children are going to write with the class, reminding the children to use the past tense, and writing key words and expressions on the board.

Ask the children to write their stories in their story books. They can illustrate their stories with suitable pictures.

Read and check the compositions with the class.

Using the Workbook

WB4 PAGE 55

1

Ask the children to complete the crossword puzzle after reading the story. Check the answers with the class.

Answers: *Down:* 1 Halloween; *Across:* 2 crunch, 3 track, 4 blood, 5 alone, 6 nervously, 7 water, 8 wander, 9 panicked, 10 strained.

2

Make the first sentence with the class then ask the children to continue on their own or in pairs. Check the answers with the class.

WB4 PAGE 56

3

Ask the children to complete the rule in pairs. Check and discuss it with the class.

4

Ask the children to find and circle six abstract nouns (do the first example with the class). Check the answers, then ask the children to complete the sentences. Check and discuss the answers with the class.

Answers: a) health, b) happiness, c) difficulty, d) fear, e) freedom, f) loneliness.

WB4 PAGE 57

5

Ask the children in pairs to look at the picture and decide which of the words they could use to describe it. Then ask them to write a description of the picture in their Workbooks. Do the first sentence with the class and write it on the board. Ask the children to read their descriptions out loud.

Extra activities and teaching aids

1 Ghost story role play

Ask the children to work in groups to write a play about a ghost and act it out for the class.

2 Scary pictures

Ask the children to draw and talk about pictures of ghosts.

3 Abstract nouns

The children could draw pictures or cut them out of magazines to illustrate abstract qualities (happiness, sadness, carelessness, etc.) and make these into a poster.

4 Group story

The class could tell a story starting: *It was a dark night ...*, with each child adding a sentence to it.

5 Dictation

It was a dark night / and two friends were coming home. / Suddenly they heard a strange sound. / It sounded like...

Ask the children to complete the story on their own.

6 Spelling check

Test the spellings of words that the children have had difficulty with in their compositions.

OBJECTIVES OF THIS UNIT
- to enable the children to evaluate persuasive writing (tourist brochure)
- to enable the children to compare places
- to develop the children's ability to use comparitives and superlatives
- to develop their ability to write a book review and to assess their own material

Language skill area	Teaching/learning strategies	Where found
Speaking and listening	Evaluating advertising material	PB1
	Talking about advertisements	PB3, Ac1
	Discussing a book, and forming an opinion	PB6, Ac3
	Dictation	Ac5
Grammar	Using comparitives and superlatives	PB4, WB1, WB2, WB3
	Recognising nouns, adjectives and adverbs	WB4, WB5, Ac4
Reading	Reading an advertisement	PB page 85, Ac1
	Answering questions about the passage	PB1
	Comparative and superlative adjectives	PB4, WB1, WB2, WB3
Spelling	Spelling check	Ac6
Writing	Writing answers to questions	PB2
	Writing a book review	PB6
	Using comparative and superlative adjectives in sentences	WB1, WB3
	Writing a tourist brochure	Ac2

KEY (All references relate to sections in this unit of the Teacher's Guide)

PB2   =   Activity 2 of Unit 20 in *Pupils' Book 4*

WB3   =   Activity 3 of Unit 20 in *Workbook 4*

Ac1   =   Activity 1 in the *Activities and teaching aids* section of this unit

UNIT 20

Using the Pupils' Book

PB4 PAGE 85

Discuss the picture with the class. Before reading, discuss the meanings of the following words and expressions: *secluded, nature-lover, spectacular.*

Ask the children to read the passage on page 85 of the Pupils' Book on their own.

PB4 PAGE 86

1

Read and discuss the questions with the class. Encourage the children to think about each adjective in (a) and decide how true it is.

2

Ask the children to write their answers in their books as full sentences, then read and check them, working in pairs. Go over the answers again orally with the class before correcting the children's writing.

3

Discuss the passage about advertisements with the class. Ask the children to suggest ways of describing their town etc. for tourists. What could they say about it? Write key words and expressions on the board. Discuss if they are true or not true.

PB4 PAGE 87

4

Read about comparing things with the class. Ask the children to practise making comparisons with real objects in the classroom, e.g. *Melissa's desk is tidier than Jamal's. Our classroom is cooler than the playground. Our classroom isn't the biggest room in the school.*

Read the adjectives in the box. Ask the children to compare the pictures using the adjectives. They can work in pairs or groups to do this. Discuss their answers with the class, then ask the children to write sentences in their books.

Read and discuss the sentences with the class.

PB4 PAGE 88

5

Read and discuss the questions with the class. Give the children time to look through the book and to decide what they think, and then to write their own opinions.

Ask the children to write their answers in their books, then add their own opinions. (Discuss these first with the class.)

Ask the children to look at their story books in pairs and decide which story was the best. Ask them to write about their best stories. Invite the children to read their best stories to the class.

Using the Workbook

WB4 PAGE 58

1

Ask the children to look at the pictures and compare them, working in pairs. Go over the answers orally with the class, then ask the children to write answers to the questions. Check and discuss the answers with the class.

Answers: a) Coconut Beach is the most crowded, b) Whitesand Beach, c) Coconut Beach, d) Pelican Beach, e) Coconut Beach.

WB4 PAGE 59

2

Do the first example with the class, then ask the children to complete the table on their own. Check and discuss the answers with the class. Ask the children to make sentences using the words.

Answers:

adjective	comparative	superlative
strange	stranger	strangest
good	better	*best*
bad	*worse*	worst
interesting	*more interesting*	*most interesting*
scary	scarier	*scariest*
funny	*funnier*	*funniest*
exciting	more exciting	*most exciting*

3

Read the example with the class and ask the children if they agree. Then ask the children to write sentences about the books in the same way, using adjectives from the table.

WB4 PAGE 60

4

Read the instructions with the class and do the first two rows of the table together. Then ask the children to work in pairs to complete the rest of the table. Read and check the answers with the class. Ask the children to use the words in sentences of their own.

Answers:
a) noisily
b) beautiful
c) peaceful   peacefully
d) graceful   gracefully
e) useful   usefully
f) healthy   healthily
g) regretful   regretfully
h) natural   naturally

5

Read and discuss the instructions and the first example with the class. Ask the children to do the rest of the exercise in pairs or groups.

   Check and discuss the answers with the class.

Answers: b) beautifully, c) peaceful, d) gracefully, e) useful, f) health, g) regretful, h) natural.

Extra activities and teaching aids

1 Reading tourist brochures

If possible, get hold of some tourist brochures which describe places the children know. Read these with the class and discuss the words that are used to describe the places, saying how truthful they think they are.

2 Writing tourist brochures

Discuss making a tourist brochure with the class. Ask them what they would need to include in it, e.g. a map, pictures, list of attractions. Ask the children to write and draw their own tourist brochures.

3 Comparing books

Ask the children to compare the books they have read recently and decide which was the most interesting, most exciting, funniest, etc. They could make an exhibition of books in the classroom, with captions showing what they thought about each of the books:

Sylvia and Amina think that this is the most interesting book they have read this year.

It is about Caribbean folktales.

4 Nouns, adjectives and adverbs

Ask the children to think of other words to add to the table in Exercise 4 of the Workbook.

5 Dictation

The most interesting book / I have read this year / is about volcanoes. / I liked the book about dinosaurs / but I thought that the book about sharks / was more exciting.

6 Spelling check

Test the spellings of words that the children have had difficulty with in their compositions.

Assessment 3

To assess the children's abilities fully, these exercises should be done with minimal guidance from the teacher. The children should also work on their own.

Check the children's work and record their performance using a chart similar to the one illustrated on page 13.

Grade the children for factually correct answers, correct use of the main grammar points, punctuation of the sentences, spelling and handwriting.

PB4 PAGE 89

Answers

1   This exercise tests the correct use of *How much...* and *How many...*
    b) How much sugar do we need?
    c) How much nutmeg do we need?
    d   How many cups of coconut do we need?
    e) How much fat do we need?
    f) How many baking trays do we need?

2   This exercise is about homophones.
    b) blew c) know/where d) write/right e) eye/sore.

PB4 PAGE 90

3   This exercise tests the ability to make adjectives from nouns by replacing the final 'e' by a 'y'.
    b) a slimy pool, c) a wavy line, d) a shady tree, e) a lacy curtain, f) a smoky fire.

4   This exercise is about synonyms.
    tasty/delicious; sour/bitter; safe/harmless; vanish/disappear; afraid/fearful; wander/stray.

5   This exercise tests the ability to identify abstract nouns.

Holidays in Trinidad and Tobago offer two very different *experiences*. There is the *excitement* and *spectacle* of Trinidad's festivals which contrast with the *peace* and natural *beauty* of Tobago. Whether it's *adventure* you want or *relaxation* T and T is the place for you!

Reading and Read Awhile books

Engaging the children's interest

A course like *Keskidee* provides a systematic programme for developing the skills necessary for the children to start to read more or less independently. However, skills alone are not enough – attitudes are also very important. There is some truth in the old maxim 'Reading is caught, not taught.'

Many teachers find that reading books to the children aloud in class – a Friday afternoon is a good time for this – is an activity that the children much enjoy, and is a good way of stimulating an interest in reading. Among the fondest schoolday memories of the authors of this book are the books their teachers read to them. It is quite common for the children to want to read the book their teacher has read to them, so teachers should try to ensure that there are copies for the children to read.

Teachers will find even at this level that there are pupils in their class who seem to have little or no interest in reading. Please do not give up on these children. Many children are late starters: and some of those who start late overtake those who seem to be ahead of them. It is almost as though different individuals have different 'clocks' inside them, and develop at different speeds. An imaginative teacher, sensitive to a child's needs, can sometimes achieve a breakthrough where none seemed possible. To help the teacher to provide varied reading material, the *Read Awhile* series has been developed to support the English textbooks used – and to develop positive attitudes to reading among even reluctant readers.

A note on grading

The books in the *Read Awhile* series are roughly graded year by year, as follows:

Blue	Level 1
Red	Level 2
Green	Level 3
Orange	Level 4
Purple	Level 5
Turquoise	Levels 6/7

However, as every teacher knows, there is an enormous variety in reading ability in the classroom. Thus while *Read Awhile* (Orange) is intended for Year 4, there will be some pupils at least who will during the course of the year want to go on to *Read Awhile* (Purple), which is intended for Year 5. On the other hand, there will be some children who still have problems with reading. If they have not read the Green books in the series originally intended for Year 3, they can do so this year.

Read Awhile books suitable for this level include:

Green (Year 3)	*Andy's Sailing Boat* *Safety at Home* *Dionne in Trouble* *Reckley's Night Journey* *Caribbean Festivals*
Orange (Year 4)	*The Magic Conch Shell* *A Boundary for Vimal* *A Challenge for Sophia* *Caribs and Arawaks* *Rainforests*
Purple (Year 5)	*Maths is Fun* *Scientists at Work* *Paulana and Tanako* *The Crab Man* *The Strange Woodcutter* *We Need Good Food*

Getting the most from the Read Awhile books

In the fourth year, *Read Awhile* books can still be used in four ways:

- they can be read with the class
- they can be read privately
- they can be stocked in a school library, and borrowed, or read in the library, as appropriate.
- they can be used as part of a class library, perhaps in a book box or cupboard.

As a class reader

We recommend that, where possible, there should be a 'class reader' in addition to a main course like *Keskidee*. Ideally, two or three class readers should be read a term, but of course this is not always possible.

This type of reading is sometimes called 'shared experience reading'. The teacher decides on a text, and every child has access to that text – ideally, a copy each, but one between two, three or even four is not uncommon. The big advantage of this kind of approach is that teachers can use the text to support core class teaching and learning activities – language and skills development – in an interesting context; pupils meanwhile have the exciting experience of reading a book, and sharing their experience of it, and experiences arising out of it, with their classmates.

Many approaches are possible, but they are all likely to be variations on the three-stage approach outlined below. These three stages are:

(a) Pre-reading

(b) While reading

(c) After reading.

(i) Pre-reading activities

In an interesting activity, the teacher introduces new or difficult words or ideas that are about to be encountered in the book. Please focus on meaning, and sound, as well as the written form. Teachers can go beyond the book at this point: for example, a poem or short story related in theme can be introduced as a gateway to the book. (For example, Grace Walker Gordon's poem 'The Arawak' could be used as a way into Paula Sorhaindo's non-fiction Orange Level book *Caribs and Arawaks* – or indeed her level 5 fiction book *Paulana and Tanako*). Using such additional texts is, of course, equally valid in the follow-up stage.

A good way to handle a book in class is for the teacher to talk about it with the class before the children begin reading it. Talk about the cover illustration, and elicit from the class what they think the book is about. Try to engage the children's imagination, and 'build bridges' with their experience, so that the books become relevant. These activities train prediction skills, and heighten anticipation.

(ii) While-reading activities

Many activities are possible:

- The teacher can read parts of the book aloud to the children. Many teachers find that it is a good idea to read the opening pages of a story to the children, and show them the pictures as they go along, to engage their interest, and reduce any initial difficulties they may have. This is a very good way to approach a book like *The Magic Conch Shell,* for example. Important words, such as names, can be written on the chalkboard.

- A book can be read in sections – part of the book in one lesson, part in another. (Children can be invited to predict what they think is going to happen in one lesson; and can be asked to recall what *has* happened in the next.)

- Teachers should treat in class particular features that the children enjoy, whether these are pictures, songs or particularly funny or exciting episodes. The most common activity is 'Comprehension questions'. Please note that too many of these can kill enjoyment; they should be restricted in the main to 'key' comprehension questions which help pupils follow the most important stages in the story, and/or character development.

- *Reading aloud* Sometimes the children can read parts of a book aloud in class. This is a good thing to do when there is dialogue, as it can be read aloud, almost like a play. *A Boundary for Vimal* lends itself to this kind of activity.

- *Dramatisation* Often, the children can dramatise the stories, using their own words. A good way to approach this is by having them read the books in pairs or groups, getting ready to act them out in class. Most fiction books lend themselves to this kind of activity.

- *'Silent reading'* Increasingly now, the children can be asked to read parts of the book on their own 'silently' – for example, simply for enjoyment, or to find out some information (a good way to use *Caribs and Arawaks,* for example) or as a preparation for reading aloud.

Many children still find it difficult to read silently, even at this stage, and 'bark at the print'. This stage is a necessary one for children to work through: they may still need to 'sound out' words to discover for themselves the sound value of the letters. So they will either whisper to themselves, or sub-vocalise. The ultimate aim is to enable them to read silently, but children will acquire this skill at different stages. While teachers should tolerate a wide range of practices by the children until they have begun to feel secure in reading, attempts should now be made to discourage reading aloud, sub-vocalising, and pointing at words in the text.

(iii) *After-reading activities*

Many of these 'follow-up' activities are suggested at the back of the *Read Awhile* books. They are designed to consolidate reading skills, develop oral and writing skills, and foster conceptual and moral development. More specific suggestions can be found on pages 93-97, when ideas for handling specific titles are explored.

Please note that successfully working through a class reader should be seen as a significant achievement, to be 'celebrated' or marked in some significant way with a serious project, mini-project, or piece of writing. In this way, a psychologically satisfying follow-up can help foster a sense of progress and achievement – and increase motivation to repeat the experience with another book.

An individual reading programme (IRS)

Whether or not a class reader is used, it can be no substitute for an individual reading programme, or an Individual Reading Scheme (IRS) as it is sometimes called. In an IRS, pupils choose books to read by and for themselves. The books on offer in an individual reading scheme should be many, and varied, both in type and in terms of reading difficulty. Many countries in the Caribbean are trying to encourage IRSs, and there can be few better ways of investing PTA funds if the school budget is too tight to invest in book boxes or the like.

An IRS can be based on a school library, but in many schools, the most practical approach is by using a book box – in effect a small mobile library. Ideally, the number of books in the book box should be rather more than there are pupils in the class, so that there is always a small 'float' of titles waiting to be read. Teachers – and the children – keep a record of books borrowed – teachers, to minimise losses and to allocate marks; the children, to gain a sense of achievement.

ERIC: the teacher's role

When operating an Individual Reading Scheme, one period a week should be spent on ERIC – 'Everyone Reading In Class' (sometimes also called USSR, which stands for 'Uninterrupted, Sustained, Silent Reading'). No one talks in ERIC lessons: the children just get on with their books. Research shows that in this kind of activity, the teacher's role is vital: the teacher acts as a role model. Each child has a book of his or her own choice; the teacher has one of his or her own choice, too. It doesn't really matter what kind of book you read, as long as it is one you enjoy. When pupils talk, or ask you questions, your response is "Save it for later. I'm trying to read my book!"

The theory is that the children will be so impressed by your dedication to the book, and by your absorption in it, that this attitude will 'rub off' on them.

The many advantages of ERIC include:

(a) the children learn through the teacher's example that reading is fun.
(b) teachers get paid to read on school time!
(c) teachers also increase their love of reading.

There are several disadvantages. One is that there is not always time to spend a whole class period on ERIC; however, even half a period is better than none. Secondly, many children do enjoy chatting about the books they are reading, and there is a lot to be said, therefore, for creating opportunities for children to talk about their reading, perhaps at the end of ERIC times.

Note that in some schools the level of noise in a classroom may be such that ERIC is too difficult to operate, and ERIL ('Everyone Reading In Library') may be more appropriate. Where no library exists, or where local conditions allow, ERIC might also be renamed ERO – 'Everyone Reading Outside.' *

Reading at home

The biggest single factor determining whether a child is successful at Common Entrance is the extent to which that child reads and studies independently. Through the PTA and informal contacts, do everything you can to encourage parents to foster reading at home. Even limited exposure to books at home can do a great deal to develop the attitudes and skills required for successful study, and reading, at school. Not every home will have suitable books, so children should be encouraged to borrow books from the book box, school or public library. If funds are limited, try an 'invisible' library scheme: each child buys one book a term or year; at the end of every week or so, each child brings in his or her book and swaps it for another.

Reader-reward schemes

Many schools have initiated some kind of 'Reading Reward Scheme', whereby pupils earn marks – or even just praise – for reading widely. Some teachers keep their own record of which books their pupils read. However, children should be encouraged to keep their own 'reading diaries', or 'logs', recording the titles and authors of books they have read, together with brief evaluative comments. Teachers should monitor these diaries, and informally ask the pupils questions about the books they list. The answers should indicate how well the children have read the book. Marks can be allocated accordingly, if desired. Later on up the school, they should write book reviews, but Year 4 is a little early for this perhaps! This year, this idea should not be pursued if the children find it burdensome: the last thing we want is to make children feel that their 'reward' for reading a book is to have to write about it! However, if they wish, the children could write very short

* The authors are indebted to the University of Reading for some of these ideas.

pieces about selected books. If desired, they could be given the following framework to complete:

Title of book ....

Author ....

Date started ....

Date completed ....

Comments ....

This book is a fiction/non-fiction book. It is about ....

I liked/disliked this book because ....

For example ....

Using the Read Awhile books

Books like those in the *Read Awhile* series can be treated in many different ways. The books should stimulate many activities that have value across the curriculum.

Detailed suggestions on how to use some of the books in the series can be found below. These suggestions are in addition to those listed at the back of each book.

Teachers should liaise with their colleague who taught the class last year, as necessary, so that ideas and books used are not duplicated. Note that, as in previous Teacher's Guides, some titles from three different levels are listed here: the 'norm', however, is likely to be books at the Orange Level.

Andy's Sailing Boat Level 3: Green – fiction

- This book raises certain questions of a moral nature including
    ◦ What can we learn from his story?
    ◦ What did Andy do that was wrong?
    ◦ Why was it wrong?
    ◦ Andy prayed that he would find the boat. On what occasions should we pray?
- Encourage the children to make their own model boats.
- Take the children to the sea, and ask them to sketch different types of boat – large and small – to make a collage or wall poster in class. They should label each type of boat. (This is a very good vocabulary development exercise.)

Caribbean Festivals Level 3: Green – non-fiction

This title should encourage the pupils to write, or do a project on, an important local festival of one kind or another – for example, a religious festival of some kind, or Chinese New Year. However, it is likely that this book was used to help to support and develop the project work suggested in *Keskidee* in Year 3. Check with the Year 3 teacher. The children could:

- research, write information pieces about, and illustrate, a wall poster or chart, telling the reader about the festival.
- design their own costumes – and then make them, even.
- if that is too ambitious, they could make suitable headdresses, or masks, for the festival.
- some children might even like to make up songs, or poems, to celebrate the festival.

If this book has not been used to support Year 3 project work, the children could follow up their reading of this book in any of the ways outlined overleaf.

- They could write true stories about what happens during the festival.

- They could draw pictures of important moments during a local festival.

- They could make up a similar story about what happened once to a child who wanted to take part in a festival such as Carnival, Cropover, Diwali, etc.

Safety at Home Level 3: Green – non-fiction

This book is really quite important, because apart from improving reading skills, it could also save lives! So if the children have not already read this book in Year 3, they should certainly do so now.

First aid, and safety at home, are very good areas for the children to do further research. If there is a school library, there should certainly be books on first aid – for example, a recent edition of the *Authorized First Aid Manual* of St John's Ambulance, British Red Cross and St Andrew's Ambulance Association (ISBN 086318 878 4). In fact, this book, or one like it, should be available in the school to help in cases of emergency.

- If the children have not already done so with *Rainforests,* use this book to teach them about how to use the Contents page and end matter:
  - The Contents page – what it is, why it is there.
  - The Index – what it is, why it is there.
  - The Glossary – what it is, why it is there.

- Set the class 'mini' research tasks, using the Contents page or Index. If you like, divide the class into groups, and set each group a different task, e.g.

- What should you do if there is a fire?

- How can you make your home safer for baby?

Teachers should make up similar 'search' questions, and make sure that the index can be used to help find the answers.

- Ask the students to design 'Safety at home' posters.

Each poster should contain just one or two simple messages – with a picture to drive the message(s) home!

Note: There are several issues raised in this book that may deserve additional attention in the classroom, either in the English lesson, or in health science or social studies. These issues are worth discussing, because they take account of the most up-to-date thinking on how to apply first aid appropriately. The issues listed below are treated in detail in *Teacher's Guide 3.*

(a) Treating cuts and scrapes
(b Choking
(c) Electric shocks
(d) Burns
(e) Hurricanes

Note: The children should be encouraged to do research on hurricanes if they have not already done so. The telephone directory may be a good source of information – for example, the Barbados Telephone Directory has excellent information on what to do in the event of a hurricane.

Among the activities on page 19 of the book is a suggestion that the children should find out more about hurricanes.

Children should draw up two lists, which could look something like this:

Dos and Don'ts during a hurricane

1   Do not leave your house or shelter during a hurricane.

2   Open one of the doors or windows of the house on the side opposite from which the wind is coming. Once the wind

changes direction, close the door or window, and open one on the opposite side.

3 If there is a lull, remain in a safe place. The wind will probably return – and may be even stronger.

Dos and Don'ts after a hurricane

1 Get medical help for anyone injured during the storm.

2 Do NOT touch loose or hanging wires.

3 Report any damage to power lines, water pipes or sewers to the police.

4 If there is a power cut, avoid eating spoiled food from the fridge.

5 Mind how you go on the road and on the pavement.

The Magic Conch Shell Level 4: Orange – fiction

Like the other books at 'Orange' level, this book is designed for fourth-year children.

The activities possible with this book could include the following.

• Introduce the children to mapwork. Help the children to find their country on the map.

• Ask the children to make a collection of different kinds of shell. (They must of course be 'dead' shells – discuss the reasons why with them.) It may be possible to organise a special outing (ideally combined with a picnic!) to the seaside to investigate some of the flora and fauna of rock pools (e.g. the 'Animal Flower Cave' in Barbados).

• Ask them to use wax crayons to draw their own underwater scenes. They can then paint over everything with blue watercolour paint.

• Show them how to do leaf prints. Children make leaf prints and fish shapes. They could even make a fish mobile!

• Give exercises on direct speech, the past tense, and the past participle, based on examples in the story.

• Ask them to draw their own map of an imaginary island, with features such as valleys, mountains, reefs, rivers, etc, each with their own made-up name

• Divide the class into groups. Each group decides where they would like the conch fairy to take them; they then do a project on that place.

• Discuss whether the children believe in fairies (or ghosts, etc.) They could act out stories of a fairy taking them to places they would like to visit – without mentioning the name of the place. The other children have to guess where the place is.

• Composition work. The children write compositions on one or more of the following topics:
  (a) My birthday party.
  (b) A gift I would like
  (c) A day in the life of a fisherman.
  (d) Imagine you are Andrea.
       Write either about your time in the sea as a fish.
       or
       Write a letter to Uncle Tom thanking him for his gift, and telling him what happened.

A Boundary for Vimal Level 4: Orange – fiction

This book will appeal to any child (boy or girl!) who loves cricket. Possible follow-up activities include:

• Find out about the national side and its performance in the Red Stripe Cup or other competition.

• Find out about, and do a wallchart on, a local cricketer. Maybe the children could interview him, or invite him to the school to give a talk.

• Discuss issues raised in the story, e.g. why did Vimal deserve his success?

• Write a composition about a recent cricket match

A Challenge for Sophia Level: Orange

Children love pets; even if they do not have one, they love to imagine what it would be like to have one. This book opens the door on many opportunities for talking and writing about pets, and doing research on how best to look after them.

The book also raises a serious issue abut whether we have any right to keep wild creatures as pets: surely, they belong to nature, not to us? The dilemma that Sophia has – whether to keep her parrot, or whether to release her into the wild – should provoke a lively discussion in class, and should raise the children's awareness of their responsibility to preserve nature for future generations.

Rainforests Level 4: Orange – non-fiction

This title provides a good support for the project on rainforests suggested in *Keskidee*. Ideally, work with another teacher – perhaps one who knows more about science, or rainforests, than you do (but perhaps *you* are the expert!). Among the possible approaches are the following:

• Read the book as a class reader, in class, and work through some of the activities suggested at the back. (But don't spend too long on it, or the subject will become boring!)

• Organise a visit to a rainforest – for example, the Moule-a-Chique rainforest in St Lucia, where you might be lucky enough to see the St Lucian Amazon parrot; or Buccament Valley in St Vincent (the St Vincent parrot and whistling warbler there are unique to St Vincent). If such a visit is out of the question, less ambitious trips might be organised, e.g. in Trinidad to the Botanic Gardens in Port of Spain.

• Prepare a list of things for the children to look for. A 'hit-list' of ten things would be ideal, e.g. particular kinds of bird, leaf-cutting ants, beetles, flowers, vines, etc. – items that the children can find, and 'tick off' on their list.

• Also provide one or two more searching questions, e.g. *Did you notice how the types of vegetation changed? Can you suggest reasons?*

• The children write about their outing, and draw a huge wall picture of a rainforest.

• The children might like to find out more about one of the animals or plants they saw or are interested in. For example, there are the birds mentioned above – and hundreds of others; in Jamaica, they might like to find out more about iguanas; in Belize, they might like to find out more about jaguars; in Guyana, they might like to find out more about caymans.

Caribs and Arawaks Level 4: Orange – non-fiction

Like *Rainforests*, this could also lay a good foundation for an outing, this time to see either sites where Amerindians used to live (including rock carvings and historic sites such as those that can be seen in Grenada (La Morne des Sauteurs) and other places), or museums or displays where their culture can be studied. Trinidad has several places that can be visited in this way, including the National Museum in Port of Spain; Jamaica and other places also have various museums and sites which are very rewarding to visit. Barbados Museum, for example, has Carib and Arawak artefacts, many dug up at Pie Corner in St Lucy.

Get the children to sketch various items that catch their eye. These sketches could become part of a wall poster or collage back at school. Grace Walker Gordon's poem 'The Arawak' could also be introduced in class at some stage while using this book.

The Crab Man Level 5: Purple – fiction

This story could be a good springboard for education about the dangers of drugs.

Paulana and Tanako Level 5: Purple –
fiction

This Trinidadian 'Romeo and Juliet' story,
about an Arawak girl and a Carib boy, will
appeal to many children. Its underlying
message is about the need for different
communities to learn to live together in
peace and harmony.

Some classes might like to develop this
story into a play: discuss with the
children how many 'scenes' they could
divide the play into. The book provides
some of the dialogue – the children could
make up the rest themselves.

Ask the children to write a story about
different communities living together in
harmony.

Scientists at Work Level 5: Purple – non-
fiction

This book is very unusual in two respects:

(a) its organising principle is the skills
and attitudes that scientists need: the
great scientists treated are examples of
these skills and attitudes in action!

(b) the book presents a non-Eurocentric
view of scientists. Of course, great
scientists such as Galileo and Marie Curie
are not ignored; but the book
acknowledges the enormous contribution
that scientists from Africa, Asia, and the
Caribbean have made to the development
of science. In the Caribbean especially,
emphasis is laid on the way Caribbean
scientists – both men and women – have
focused on resolving the problems that
ordinary people have to face in their
everyday lives, whether they be farmers,
fishermen – or just 'the man in the street,
the woman in the yard'. In this way, the
book fosters a 'can do' attitude among our
youth.

The children could choose any one of
the scientists mentioned, and find out
more about him or her.

Some of the books in the Read Awhile series

A range of Caribbean writers and storytellers – both new and established, and representing a broad selection of islands – have contributed towards the *Read Awhile* series. From Barbados there are Allison Douglas and Osmonde Douglas; from Jamaica come Jean D'Costa and Sybil Seaforth; writer and artist Edgar Arnette represents The Bahamas; and there is Esther O'Neale from Grenada, Dorothy Jolly and Paula Sorhaindo from Dominica, and Sheila Williams from St Maarten, while Trinidad and Tobago are represented through the writings of Cherryl Bradshaw, Annette Charles, Earl Lovelace, Faustin Charles and Annette Commissiong, and St Lucia by Patricia Phillip.

For more information about the *Read Awhile* series, contact your local Longman representative, or check with your local bookshop.

Blue
(Level 1)

Sun, Moon and Water
The Cricket Bat
The Moon in my Room

Red
(Level 2)

How the Donkey got his Bray
Animal Rhymes
Crawfie the Crapaud

Green
(Level 3)

Reckley's Night Journey
Andy's Sailing Boat
+Caribbean Festivals
+Safety at Home
Dionne in Trouble

Orange
(Level 4)

The Magic Conch Shell
A Boundary for Vimal
+Caribs and Arawaks
+Rainforests
A Challenge for Sophia

Purple
(Level 5)

Paulana and Tanako
The Crab Man
+We Need Good Food
The Cloud that Lost its Silver Lining
+Maths is Fun
The Strange Woodcutter
+Scientists at Work

Turquoise
(Levels 6/7)

The Search
Caesar and the Three Robbers
Duppy Tales
+Our Planet, Our Home

+ indicates that the title is non-fiction.

Notes

Notes